MAGAHĪ PHONOLOGY
A Descriptive Study

About the Author

Dr. Saryoo Prasad, M.A., Ph.D. was born on the 13th March, 1934 in Bihar, Nalanda. He did M.A. in Hindi and awarded Ph.D. from Patna University on a Significant subject of Modern Linguistics "A Descriptive Study of Magahi Phonology" in 1966. He served as a Lecturer in B.R.S. College, Banka, Bhagalpur University and Nalanda College, Bihar Sharif, Magadh University, Bodh Gaya and lastly rendered his valuable sevices as the founder Director-*cum*-Principal of Nalanda Research Institute and College, Bihar Sharif. He had been also the editor of its renowned research quarterly journal "*Shodh*" for several years.

Dr. Prasad has published a number of research paper in the Journals of repute on different topics of Modern Linguistics, Literature and Culture. He has Several honours to his credit, one of them "Vidya Vachaspati" conferred on him by Vikramshila Hindi Vidyapeeth, Bhagalpur. He has invited on several occasions of national and international seminars to present his valuable research papers on significant topics.

The Government of Bihar, Department of Human Resource Development has nominated him as a honorable member in its prominent academic institutions for several terms.

As a specialist of Modern Linguistics he has been invited to deliver his valuable lecturers on the methods and problems of "Linguistic Survey of Bihar" for a week long session, organised by Government of Bihar and Bihar Rashtra Bhasha Parishad jointly.

The World renowned Scholar of several languages Maha Pandit Rahul Sankrityayan has appraised him as a great nature Poet of Magahi in "*Hindi Sahitya ka Vrihat Itihas*", Volume XVI, published by Nagari Pracharni Sabha, Kashi.

MAGAHĪ PHONOLOGY

A Descriptive Study

Saryoo Prasad

CONCEPT PUBLISHING COMPANY, NEW DELHI-110059

Cataloging in Publication Data—DK
Courtesy: D.K. Agencies (P) Ltd. <docinfo@dkagencies.com>

Prasad, Saryoo, 1934-
Magahī phonology : a descriptive study / Saryoo Prasad.
p. cm.
Includes bibliographical references (p.)
Includes index.
ISBN 13: 9788180695254
ISBN 10: 8180695255

1. Magahi language—Phonology. I. Title.

DDC 491.454 759 22

ISBN-13: 978-81-8069-525-4
ISBN-10: 81-8069-525-5

First Published 2008

Published and Printed by
Ashok Kumar Mittal
Concept Publishing Company
A/15-16, Commercial Block, Mohan Garden
New Delhi-110 059 (India)

Phones : 25351460, 25351794
Fax : 091-11-25357103
Email : publishing@conceptpub.com

To

The Memory of

My Punyashlok Father

Govind Sahu

PREFACE

This book is intended to analyse the phonological systems, patterns and structure of Magahi according to the canon of Modern Descriptive Lingustics. The whole research has been conducted in Deccan College Post-Graduate and Research Institute, Poona, an advance centre of Lingustics in India, under the invaluable guidence of Dr. A.M. Ghatage, an eminent scholar of Modern Linguistics and Head of the Post-Graduate Department of Linguistics, Poona University, Pune.

When I got M.A. (First Class) in Hindi from Patna University, I had been advised by Acharya Nalinvilochan Sharma, a renowned scholar of Hindi critisim (then Head of the Department of Hindi, Patna University) to carry on research on a subject of importance in Modern Linguistics on Magahi Phonology. I had been registered in Patna University on the subject "A Descriptive Study of Magahi Phonology" under Dr. Raja Ram Rastogi (Prof. in the Department of Hindi, Patna University). During the period, I was awarded a research scholarship by UGC to carry on research on the above subject for the requisite number of terms.

But it was not possible to carry research on this specific subject in Patna University as there was no proper environment and facilities available so far as Modern Linguistics is concerned. Even not only in Patna University, but there was no research methodology and sufficient guidance available in the northern universities of India, specially, in this subject. As such, I was sent by the Department of Hindi to Deccan College Post-Graduate and Research Institute, Pune.

I met there Dr. S.M. Katre, a renowned scholar of Linguistics in India and the then Director and Professor in Deccan College Post-Graduate and Research Institute. He extended me all the research facilities and invaluable guidance including library, hostel and mess of the Institute. He has allotted my study room just in the right side of the historical study room of Lokmanya Balgangadhar Tilak, a famous Scholar, Editor and the Hero of the independence movement of India as he had been also a student of one of the oldest colleges in our country. His immemorable study room has been still preserved for the visitors, scholars and students of different parts of India and abroad also. It was my rare opportunity that my entire work has been completed in my study room. I had been attended there several post-graduate and diploma classes of Linguistics and had undergone necessary training in Linguistics which was essential for this work.

This book has been devided into three sections and nine chapters. The first section of the book deals with Segmental Phonems of Magahī consists of Vowels, Pure Vowels, Diphthongs, Nasalization of Vowels, classification of Vowels, their description and distribution. Diphthongs of the language have also been analysed along with their contrasts, Phonological structure, distribution, Phonetic Features and their position on Cordinal Vowel Diagram. Apart from this, the Sequence of Vowels has also been described on the basis of their types, Phonetic features and distribution.

In the coming chapters consonants have been undertaken analyzing their classifications, Phonetic and Phonemic Characters, Classification, Contrast, Position and Formation class including their allophones. Then the clusters of Magahi have been described consisting of their types, Medial and Final clusters, two and three consonant clusters etc.

Chapter Five covers the syllabic structure with syllabic patterns and divisions. In this context, the frequency has also been described following the nature of texts, result and conclusion.

The second section of the book opens with the Supra-Segmental Phonemes pertaining Nasalization, Independent and Dependent Nasalization Allophonic features and Morphemic characteristics along with Prosodic nature.

Chapter seven provides a study of the Junctures of the language including the nature of Transition and kinds of Juncture contrast, phonetic features, stress and Morthological boundries.

On the other hand, Chapter Seventh deals with the Intonation of Magahi describing its basic elements, four pitch levels and two terminal contours, their contrasts, basic elements, stress, distributional position and division of macro segments.

Chapter Eighth analyses the Acoustic elements of the language along with survey of the Wave Forms, Specific Character of Pitch Levels (PLs) and Terminal contours (TCs). Description of Pitch Levels and Terminal contour, the Nature of Rising and Falling TCs. describing Four PLs and wave forms.

The Third Section deals with the Componential Analysis following the distinctive features, classification and their types.

In the second chapter of the book, an Inventory of the Phonemes of Magahī has already been included and these are classified as Segmental and Supra Segmental Phonemes consisting of Nasalization, Juncture, Intonation, Pitch levels and Terminal Contours.

All the findings, facts and figures have been tabularized here also into nine tables only by which the scholars and students of linguistics shall be enable to visualize the full spectrum of Magahī Phonology. Apart from the minute observations and detailed analysis of Magahī Phonology, some significant Bibliogaphy and Indexes have also been added in the last.

In the preparatioin of the thesis I feel indebted to Dr. A.M. Ghatage, Dr. Raja Ram Rastogi and Dr. S.M. Katre, who always paved my way during my work. I am indebted to Dr. L.M. Khubchandani, who also went through the draft of the thesis and made some valuable suggestions whereas I have been benefited from the discussions on my problems with Dr. P.B. Pandit, Dr. A.R. Kelkar and Dr. M.L. Apte, all of them were the professors and readers of Modern Lingustics in Deccan College Post-Graduate and Research Institute. My thanks are due to Professor C.R. Sankaran who extended all the laboratory facilities and helped me in acoustic analysis.

I owe gratitude to Prof. Siddheswar Prasad, Ex. Honorable Governor of Tripura and Prof. Guru Prasad (Head of the Department of Hindi, K.L.S. College, Nawada and member of the Senate, Magadh University, Bodh Gaya) from whom I always got constant inspirations and encouragements.

I am also obliged to the authorities of UGC, New Delhi who accorded on me a Research Scholarship during the period of my research.

It is my pious duty to express my gratitude to my late respected father Punyashlok Govind Sahu who always inspired me to achieve the highest goal of education.

On this auspicious occasion of the publication of this book, my thanks are also due to Mr. Ashok Kumar Mittal and S.K. Sinha, the proprietor and executive of Concept Publishing Company, New Delhi who are publishing it with all professional cares.

I will not forget, at this time, my such friends, students, scholars and professors who constantly demanded immediate publication of this book. I am confident, the publication of this book will be highly welcomed on wide scale by the Professors, Scholars and Students of linguistics. I hope, the next edition of this book will come soon.

Basant Panchmi,
The 23rd January, 2007

Dr. Saryoo Prasad
Director-cum-Principal,
Nalanda Research Institute
and College, Station Road,
Bihar Sharif, Nalanda-803101.

LIST OF ABBREVIATIONS

Asp.	Aspirated
C.	Consonant
C/S.	Cycles Per Second
Chap.	Chapter
diph.	Diphthong
e.g.	For example
fig.	Figure
fric. conts.	Frictionless Continuants
i.e.	That is
J.R.A.S.	Journal of Royal Asiatic Society
L.S.I.	Linguistic Survey of India
P.L.	Pitch Level
Tab.	Table
T.C.	Terminal Contour
V.	Vowel
V.S.	Vikramī Saṁvat
vd.	Voiced
vl.	Voiceless
vol.	Volume
vs.	Versus

CONTENTS

Section III
COMPONENTIAL ANALYSIS

1

INTRODUCTION - I

Purpose and Scope

This study is intended to provide a detailed analysis of the phonological structure of Magahī, in terms of articulatory components, of auditory qualities and of acoustic properties. The entire analysis consists of three sections, *i.e.*, (1). Segmental Phonemes, (2). Supra-segmental Phonemes and (3). Componential analysis. The acoustic analysis is confined only to the intonation structure of the language.

This is, perhaps, the first effort to analyse in such detail the significant phonological elements of a dialect of Hindi speaking region, according to the canons of descriptive Linguistics.

Name of the Dialect

Magahī is one of the dialects of Bihar belonging to the Indo-Āryan Group. Grierson has named the Western Magadhī languages as Bihārī which contains Magahī, Maithilī and Bhojapuri.[1] By this term Grierson wanted to recognise the wide spoken languages of Bihar which seems to be more convenient, nothing else.

Magahī or Magadhī is essentially the language of Magadh. Even now it is called Magadhī by some educated people, but of course more current modern name is Magahī, phonemically that is transcribed as /məgəhi/.

The Glory of Magadha

Magadha has played an important role in the History of India.

The oldest Magadha was considered as the District of Patna along with the Northern half of the District of Gaya. The oldest capital of Magadha was at Rājgir where Jarāsandha, Bimbisāra and Ajātaśatru showed their bravery. Rājgir and Nālandā were the main places where Buddha and Tīrthaṅkara Mahāvīra often used to stay. Nālandā, one of the oldest universities of the world, has a glorious background, built by the mightily emperors and the cultural organisers of Magadha. The great Aśoka, third century B.C., ruled over a wider portion of India and Afghanistan.

It should be noticed that at first a regional language got great honour in the country of Magadha.[2] Buddha delivered his religious teachings in the language of Magadha, the oldest form of Magadhī.[3]

Under Mohammedans the capital was shifted from Patna to the town of Bihar Sharif, in the south of the Patna District. The town of Bihar was the city of Buddhist monastery on account of which the whole state was called Bihar.

During the British administration upto the year 1865 the greater part of the present Paṭna District and the North of the present Gaya District, which contained the original region of oldest Magadha, was recognised as 'Zila Bihar' on one hand and the rest of Gaya (South Gaya) and the portion of Hazaribagh District being known as 'Zila Ramgarh' on the other hand.

Linguistic Boundaries of Magahī

At present Magahī is not confined to the old boundary of Magadha. It is spoken not only in the District of Gaya and Patna but also in the Districts of Hazaribagh, on the west in a portion of the District of Palamau and on the east in portions of the Districts of Monghyr and Bhagalpur.

Magahī is spoken over nearly the area of fourteen thousand square miles.[4] On its eastern frontier Magahī meets Bengali where it is not so pure. Grierson has named the dialect of this region as Eastern Magahī.[5] It is found in South-East Hazaribagh, in Manbhum, in the South-East of the District of Ranchi, in Kharaswan and even so far South as Mayūrabhañja and Bamra which have been merged into Bengal after states reorganisation between Bihar and Bengal. It is also spoken in the west of the District of Malda.

Pure Magahī is spoken mostly all over its region. It is not observed only in its western parts, *i.e.*, Patna, Gaya, Hazaribagh, Monghyr and Bhagalpur but even in its eastern parts, *i.e.*, in the south of the District of Ranchi and in the north of the District of Singbhum and in Saraikela and Kharaswan.

On the north, Magahī is bounded by the various forms of Maithilī which is now called 'Bajjikā', across the Ganges. On the west, it is bounded by Bhojapurī speaking areas, the Districts of Shahabad and Palamau. On the North-East and East it is bounded by the Chhikachhiki Maithilī, which is now called 'Aṅgikā', of Monghyr, Bhagalpur and the Santhāla Parganās, on the South-East, by the Bengali of Manbhum and East Singhbhum. On the other hand, the Plateau of Ranchi is bounded on its three sides (the North, the East and the South) by a belt of a population of Magahī speakers.

Number of Speakers

On the basis of the census of 1881, Grierson mentioned the total number of Magahī speakers 6,504,817.[6] But the census of 1951, shows much reduced number of Magahī speakers, that is only 3,728.[7] On the other hand according to the census of 1961 the number of Magahī speakers is 3,792,447.[8]

In the Constitution of India, Bihar is east frontier of Hindi speaking region. Owing to cultural and literary solidarity Magahī people consider themselves as Hindi speakers and for that particular reason they report 'Hindi' as their mother tongue in the census. They could not write 'Magahī' as their mother tongue and 'Hindi' (khaṛībolī) as their second language. It is carried on not only by Magahī people but also by Bhojapurī and Maithilī people. In all, therefore, only one lakh of people have reported their mother tongue as 'Bihārī'. But it does not mean that the number of Magahī speakers have been reduced to such extent. As a matter of fact, the number of Magahī speakers has been growing on day to day together with the increasing population of India. To get the approximate number of Magahī speakers, however, some guesses have been made as under :

Today, as a rough data, it has been crossed the population of even two crores.[9,10]

Dialects

Grierson has divided the language into two parts, standard Magahī and Eastern Magahī as mentioned above. Though the standard Magahī does not have further sub-dialects, however, some variations might be observed. But Eastern Magahī shows at least its five varieties which are[11]—(1). Kuṛmali or Kurmali[12] of Manbhum and Mayūrbhañja, (2). Sadrikol of Bamra, (3). So-called 'Bengali' of Hazaribagh, (4). Panch-Pargania or Tamaria of Ranchi and (5). Khottai of Malda. Of these Kurmali of Manbhum varies a lot from the Kurmali of Mayūrbhañja.

Origin

Magahī is the successor of Magadhī, as it is quite evident by the term Magahī or Magadhī. Of course 'Magahī' is derived from 'Magadhī' but to reach its present name it had to go through a long process which may be mentioned as in,

मागधी > मागही[13] > मगही

It is assumed that at first Magadha had changed as Magaha (present name) and then the language of it came as Magahī.

In the oldest Buddhist literature Pāli was referred again and again as Magadhī, the language of Buddha.[14] The historical and cultural evidence also reveals that Magadha contributed a lot in the formation of Pāli.[15] Kaccayana, the earliest grammarian of Pāli called it as Magadhī.[16]

The present form of Magahī shows much more similarity to Pāli rather than other middle Indo-Āryan languages. Not only on the basis of vocabulary and Phonetics, but even on the basis of grammar Magahī shows its deep relation with Pāli.[17] On the other hand it seems very far from the so-called Magadhī Prākrit which was, as a matter of fact, an artificial language.[18] Magahī is, in respect to similarity, much nearer to Ardha Magadhī than Magadhī[19] Prakrit.

Literature

Generally, it is believed that Magahī has no literature. But now we have secured such evidence which brings many literary works, still unpublished, to light.[20]

Magahī literature starts from Siddha saints, those belong to Vrajayāna school, that is a corrupt form of Buddhism.[21] It cannot be ignored that Nālandā, Udautapuri and Vikramaśilā were the main centres of Siddhas and their entire literature was written in the language of those places, *i.e.*, oldest Magahī.[22] From the point of phonetics, grammar and vocabulary the language of Siddha literature is quite similar to present Magahī.[23]

During 1200 AD. to 1400 AD. there are many Sant poets who have written a vast religious literature. Of them some names may be cited here : Dharam Das, Badri Das (Salimpur, Patna), Chandan Das and Amrit Das (Jahanabad, Gaya), Baba Kadam Das, Sohang Das and Hemnath Das.[24]

Apart from the religious literature, mentioned above, a number of folk tales, ballads and popular songs have been handed down for centuries from mouth to mouth. Strolling bards recite the ballads and songs in this dialects.

At present, also there are some renowned poets and writers of Magahī who have been contributing nice literary pieces. A few periodicals are also published in the language.

Thus, the whole Magahī literature can be divided into three heads : Siddha Period (from 800 AD. to 1200 AD.), Sant Period—later Siddha period (from 1200 AD. to 1400 AD.) and Modern Period (from 1400 AD. to present days).

Influences on Magahī

There are mostly '*tadbhav*' words, however, in the speech of Brāhmaṇs and educated people some Sanskrit words may be found frequently. Owing to the influence of Mohammedans many words have been derived from Persian and Arabic which are widely used. In the speech of educated class some English words are being used with greater frequency. Magahī is very much influenced by the Khaṛībolī, as a result of its close contact with standard Hindi. Inspite of the various influences Magahī has not accepted many changes on its phonological and grammatical structure.

Orthography

Kaithi is the script generally used for Magahī. The community of businessman also use Mahājani script in their trades. But at present Devanāgarī is the common script of Magahī people for correspondence, business, literary works and periodicals.

Informants

The present analysis is entirely based on the speech of the writer of these lines. I was born at Bihar Sharif, a historical town of Bihar State and I speak standard Magahī as my mother tongue. I was educated in Bihar Sharif upto degree standard through the medium of Hindi and English. I left my native place for post-graduate study in Hindi and had been to Patna for a considerable period. Though Patna is a Magahī speaking area, however, it is a cosmopolitan city. After completing my M.A. I joined a degree college in the Maithilī region in the Department of Hindi as a lecturer. I have spent some time in the different parts of India, especially in Delhi, Agra and Calcutta. I had a close contact with Marāṭhī, Bhojapurī, Maithilī and Awadhī speakers. Afterwards I went to Poona for research and lived there for nearly two years.

Though the entire study is based on my own speech at least

three to four times I have checked my whole data with the help of some uneducated native speakers of Magahī.

REFERENCES

1. *LSI.,* Vol. V, Part II, G.A. Grierson, 1903, p. 30.
2. *Indo-Aryan and Hindi,* S.K. Chatterji, 1960, p. 64.
3. *Ibid.*, p. 178.
4. *Magahī Sanskar Geet*, Dr. Vishwanath Prasad, 1962, p. 2.
5. *LSI.*, Vol. V, Part II, p. 31.
6. *LSI.*, Vol. V, Part II, p. 34.
7. *Census of India*, 1951, Language Vol.
8. *Census of India*, 1961, Volume I, Part II, Annexure III CCXXXV.
9. *Magahī Sanskar Geet*, Dr. Vishwanath Prasad, 1962, p. 2.
10. *Magahī Vyakaran Kosh*, Dr. Sampatti Aryani, 1965, p. 20.
11. *LSI.*, Vol. V, Part II, pp. 145-180.
12. *Kurmali Bhasha aur Sahitya*, Dr. Vishwanath Prasad, 1960. Bihar Rashtrabhasha Parishad, Patna.
13. In the Jain Canon '*Samvayang Sutta*' (6-7th cent. AD.)
    'अद्ध मागही भासा' or 'अद्ध मगहीय' words are used.
14. (a) *Visuddhi Magga*, Part, 14.
    (b) *Chulla Vagga*, Aṭṭha Kathā-5, 33, 1.
    (c) *Chulla Vaṁsa*–37, 230, 242, 4.
    (d) *Abhidhānapadipikā*.
    (e) *Vinayabinichāya Ṭikā*.
15. *Magahī Sanskar Geet*, Dr. Vishwanath Prasad, 1962, pp. 7-8.
16. सा मागधी मूल भासा नराया आदि कप्पिका।
    ब्राह्मणा चस्सुता लापा संबुद्धा चापि भासि रे।।
17. *Magahī : Udgam tatha Vikas*, Saryoo Prasad, *'Parishad Patrika'*, Bihar Rashṭra Bhasha Parishad.
18. *Indo-Āryan and Hindi*, S.K. Chatterji, 1960, p. 96.
19. *Magahī : Udgama tatha Vikas,* Saryoo Prasad.
20. *Magahī : Udgam tatha Vikas*, Saryoo Prasad.
21. *Ganga Puratatvank*, Rahul Sankrityana, p. 234.
22. (a) Ibid.
    (b) *Bihar Through the Ages*, R.R. Diwakar, 1958, pp. 355-357.
23. *Magahī : Udgam tatha Vikas*, Saryoo Prasad.
24. (a) *Ibid.*
    (b) *Magahī Sanskar Geet*, Dr. Vishwanath Prasad, 1962, p. 29.

INTRODUCTION - II

Phonology is an integral part of Linguistics without which a complete conception and study of any language of the world can't be possible. As a matter of fact, language is a most valuable single possession of human being. Everyone in every walk of life is deeply concerned with language in a practical way for we make use of it in everything we do.

Phonology is a kind of signalling via sound. In the study of Phonology of a language the sounds and differences between them have one and only one function in the language to keep utterence apart. The phonemes of a language are such elements which stand in contrast with each other in the phonological system of a language.

The book is an elementary practical account of that branch of modern descriptive linguistics, which is concerned with spoken sounds, the phonetics and phonemics of Magahi. This is virtually the only basic work of one of the sub-languages of Hindi speaking region of north India, Magahi, which provides a complete account of physiological phonetics and of the phonemics on the basis of contrast through detailed analysis and minutest observations of experimental and acoustic phonetics and machine analysis.

When the whole Europe was not acquainted with the name of science of language and grammar, India had already developed it about 6th to 7th century B.C.

The oldest monuments of human wisdom and knowledge is Ṛgveda which has been regarded as the scriptures of God. That's why the four Vedas have been recognised and honoured as "APURUSHEYA", not written by human beings but by God. In this perspective, the whole emphasis was laid down on correct utterance and pronounciation of the hymns of ṚgVeda including the other three *Vedas, Ayur, Sam* and *Atharva*. Therefore, strict rules and regulations have been made for their correct utterance and pronounciation. It was believed that if any mistake occurred in recitation of the hymns of *Vedas* the meaning and effect will be changed which will amount to a grave sin and both the reciter and listeners will have to suffer a lot. The hymns of *Vedas* are generally prayers to Almighty God and are recited on auspicious occasions, especially during the time of *yagyas*.

The most significant and historical contribution in the field of science of languages was "*Ashtadhyayi*" written by the great Maharshi Pāṇini. As a matter of fact, this was the only scientific descriptive as-well-as perfect grammar of any language of the world based on the contemporary Sanskrit, spoken widely all over India as "Lingua Franca".

Pāṇini has divided his "*Ashtadhyayi*" into eight chapters as it is apparent from its very name and it incorporates four thousand "*Sutras*". Actually Pāṇini was a great saint who led a very disciplined life and remained engaged in constant "*Tapasya*". As a result he got fourteen *Maheshwar Sutras* with the grace of Lord Shiva. In the fourteen "*Maheshwar Sutras*" he described the organs of speech and their points of articulations. He classified all the vowels and consonants in different categories recognising their utterance characters. It was customary for *brahmins* to get by heart the Vedic hymns and recite them on auspicious occasions in a correct fashion.

Pāṇini also established that each and every word has its own root, which was called "*Dhatu*". Apart from that, he drew a sharp line of division between "*Chhandas*", the language of Vedas and contemporary Sanskrit, spoken widely all over India during that time. One of the main characteristics of "*Ashtadhyayi*" is its brevity as the "Sutras" are the shortest form of expression.

From the available sources, it has been assumed that Maharshi Pāṇini had travelled all over India and had surveyed the spoken form of his contemporary Sanskrit on a wide scale with minute observations. He found vast differences of the spoken forms of Sanskrit from place to place. He, therefore, disciplined and tightened the whole grammar of Sanskrit with his strict rules and regulations. As a result after Pāṇini no one could dare even touch it with any correction and addition. As Latin and Greek have ceased to be living languages, Sanskrit has met the same fate. But inspite of this fact, Sanskrit still exists as our cultural value and inspires our literature, Philosophy, religion and our behaviour and standards of life.

From the above facts it can be seen that India had achieved excellent success in the field of Linguistics even in seventh century B.C. Various kinds of Phonetic disciplines and books are found, which were called "*Shiksha*" and "*Pratishakhya*". So far as the "*Shiksha*" books are concerned, their numbers are not less than eighty. Some of them the prominent shiksha books may also be mentioned here :

"Amresh Shiksha", "Lomashi Shiksha", "Pratishakhya Pradeep Shiksha", "Yagyawalkya Shiksha", "Nardiya Shiksha", "Katyayeni Shiksha", "Gautami Shiksha", "Sadashsloki Shiksha", "Parashari Shiksha", "Bhardwaj Shiksha", "Sonikya Shiksha", "Vashishta Shiksha", "Pāṇiniya Shiksha", "Vyas Shiksha", "Valmikya Shiksha" etc. Apart from these Shiksha books there were seven to eight Pratishakhya books. They follow as under: "Ṛgveda Pratishakhya", "Vajashneyi Pratishakhya", "Taitireya Pratishakhya", "SamVeda Pratishakhya", "Atharva Veda Pratishakhya", "Riktantra" and "Chaturdhyapika" etc.

Originally these shiksha books were based on the theoretical principles of sound study,while the Pratishakhyas were the most practical methods of utterances of different Vedas and their branches. In this respect Dr. Siddheswar Verma and Allen have provided detailed informations in their famous books on the phonetics of ancient India.

Before Pāṇini, Muni Yask had written his famous book "*Nighantu*" pertaining the meanings of the words of Vedas which may be regarded as the first work of Semantic. After Muni Yask several grammarians had come up. Pāṇini himself had referred in his "*Ashtadhyayi*" to the school of "Udichya" and "Prachya" along with some famous grammarians as Apishali, Kashyapa, Gargeya and so on. According to "*Taitireya Samhita*" (7-4-7) there was also a renowned grammarian Indra whose school was continued even after Pāṇini. Katyayana was also belonged to Indra school. Though, Katyayana had criticised Pāṇini in his "*Vartika*", but that was owing to the gap of time and the changes occurring between Pāṇini and Katyayana. Instead of the criticism of Pāṇini and Katyayan had provided a helpful study in favour of interpretations of "*Ashtadhyayi*". "*Vajasneyi Pratishakhya*" was also assumed as the writing of Katyayana.

In the second century B. C. Maharshi Patanjali, one of the prominent grammarian of Sanskrit has deeply interprated the Sutras of "*Ashtadhyayi*" in his masterpiece book "*Mahabhashya*". He had strongly defended and established Maharshi Panini and vehemantly criticised Katyayana. Apart from this in his "*Mahabhashya*" Patanjali had broadly interprated the Philoshpy of language, which has been recognized as a great contribution of Patanjali. Considering the historical contribution of Pāṇini, Katyayana and Patanjali they have regarded as "*Munitreya*", the three saints of grammarians.

The details about the life of Pāṇini have not been fully discovered, but he is supposed to have belonged to the place of Atak (Salapur), now in Lahor in Pakistan, after the partition of India. He was a Udichya Brahmin. His mother's name was known as "Akshi". Pāṇini had been examined at Patliputra, one of renowned centres of education and linguistics in ancient India. He was a student of Upversha, who had also been examined at Patliputra as it is evident from a *shloka* of "*Kavya Mimansha*", the famous book of a great critic Rajshekhar. Not only Pāṇini but Verruchi, Upvarsha, Versha and Patanjali were also the students of that prominent centre of education and linguistics:

> *"Shruyate Patliputre shastrakar Priksha atrope*
> *Varsha Vershawih Pāṇini*
> *Punglavih Vyadih Ver ruchi, Patanjali ih Prikshita*
> *Kyapimup jagmuh."*

Pāṇini wrote his grammar on purely descriptive methods on the basis of the spoken forms of his contemparary Sanskrit. Virtually Pāṇini was the basic thinker, philosopher as well as the propounder of Modern Descriptive Linguistics which developed in Europe after a long gap in the nineteenth and twentieth centuries. Truly speaking, Bloomfield, the main philosopher, theoritician and builder of Modern Descriptive linguistics has broadly accepted the historical contribution of Pāṇini in his monumental book "*Language*", published at first in January 1933 at Chicago. In "*Language*" he has widely accepted:

> "It was in India, however, that there arose a body of knowledge which was destined to revolutionize European ideas about language. The Brahmine religion guarded, as sacred texts some very ancient collection of hymns, the oldest of these collections the Rig-Veda, dates in part, at a conservative estimate, from about 1200 B.C. As a language of these texts grew antiquated, the proper way of pronouncing them, and their correct interpretation, become the task of a special class of learned man. The antiquarian interest in language which arose in this way, was carried over into a practical sphere. Among the Hindus, as among us, different classes of society differed in speech. Apparently there were forces at work which led upper class speakers to adopt lower class forms of speech. We find the Hindu grammarians extending their interest from the scriptures to the upper caste language, and making rules and lists of forms descriptive of the correct type of speech which they called Sanskrit. In time they workedout a systematic arrangement of grammar and lexicon. Generations of such labour must have preceded the writing of the oldest treatise that have come down to us, grammar of Panini."

Bloomfield has again emphathecised on the unique contribution of Pāṇini and broadly accepted :

> "This grammar, which dates from somewhere round 350 to 250 B.C., is one of the greatest monuments of human inteligence. It describes, with the minutest detail, every inflection, derivation, and composition, and every syntactic usage of its author's speech. No other language, to this day, has been so perfectly described. It may have been due, inpart, to this excellent codification that Sanskrit became, in time, the official and literary language of all of Brahmin India. Long after it had ceased to be spoken as any one's native language, it remained (as classical Latin remained in Europe) the artificial medium for all writings on learned or religious topics."

He further said "some knowledge of Sanskrit and of the Hindu grammar had reached Europe, through missionaries, in the sixteenth and seventeenth centuries. In the eighteenth century, Englishmen in India transmitted more exact reports; round the beginning of the nineteenth century, the knowledge of Sanskrit became part of the equipment of European scholars.

The Indian grammar presented to European eyes, for the first time, a complete and accurate description of a language, based not upon theory but upon observation. Moreover, the discovery of Sanskrit disclosed the possibility of a comparative study of languages.

To begin with, the concept of related languages was strikingly confirmed by the existence, in far-off India, of a sister of the familiar languages of Europe; witness for example, the Sanskrit equivalent of the words......

Even more important was the insight into linguistic structure which one got from the accurate and systematic Hindu grammar. Up till now, one had been able to see only vague and fluid similarities, for the current grammars, built on the Greek model, did not clearly set off the features of each language. The Hindu grammar tought Europeans to analyze speech-forms; when one compared the constituent parts, the resemblances, which hitherto had been vaguely recognized, could be set forth with certainty and precision".[1]

Actually, Leonard Bloomfield was a basic theoretician and fundamental Philosopher of Science of Language. He had studied several languages of world including Sanskrit. He was a professor of Germanic Philology in the University of Chicago. Bernard Block, one of the famous linguists, in his tribute to Bloomfield, very truly wrote in the prominent journal "*Language*"— "There can be no doubt that Bloomfield's greatest contribution to the study of language was to make a science of it."[2] Exactly, this is an accurate judgement. His landmark book "*Language*", first of all introduced and established "Modern Descriptive Linguistics" along with all the aspects of language study, i.e., Phonetics, Phonemics, Morphology, Syntex, Semantics, Dilectology, Grammatical forms and Comparative methods etc. Including all the aspects of linguistic analysis, Bloomfield explained fully and differenciated the elements, Phonemics and Phonetics, an important part of linguistics. The most outstanding book of Bloomfield, as a matter of fact, has revolutionized the entire world of linguistic study with help of this book, a clearcut conception of linguistics has been drawn before the scholars, students and interested persons in this field. As such, the complete atmoshphere of the science of language has been entirely changed and deep impact of Bloomfield has influenced generation to generations, continued so many years. As such, the first half of the 20th century has been called "the Era of Bloomfield". The deep vision and very wide conceptions of Bloomfield has truly recognized "*Ashtadhyayi*" of the great Pāṇini as "one of the greatest monuments of human intelligence". In this respect, I would again like to quote Bernard Block, the renouned professor of Linguistics at Yale University and long time editor of the famous journal "*Language*" and also a colleague of Bloomfield :

> "It is not too much to say that every significant refinement of analystic method produced in this country since 1933 has become as a direct result of the impetus given to linguistic research by Bloomfield's book. If today our methods are in some ways better than his, if we see more clearly that he did himself certain aspects of structure that he first revealed to us, it is because we stand upon his shoulders."[3]

If the nineteenth century was the age of historical and comparative linguistics, then the twentieth century may be said the golden age of Modern Descriptive Linguistics.

In the first phase of twentieth century a fundamental theoritician Swiss Ferdinand de Saussure (1857-1913) contributed a new conception of modern linguistics. His lectures were collected, edited and published after his death by two of his students, themselves, famous scholars Charles Bally and Albert Sechehaye under the title "*Course de Linguistique ge'nerale*", published later on in English also by Wade Baskin in the name of "*Course in General Linguistics*" from New York in 1959.

Saussure's great service to the study of language was in a series of clearcut distinctions and definitions which he made about the nature and forms of language. He defind the subject as "Parole" (utterance) and "Lingue" (Language). Language leads a dual existence. First of all there is a flow of living speech. This is personalized language—your speech and my speech. Saussure had catogorised it as "Parole" which is a physical reality that varies from man to man. But another aspect of language which he called "Langue". As "Langue" is an abstract of linguistic system exists quite apart from the individual. "Langue" is not spoken by anybody, but a composite body of linguistic phenomena. It is essence of a social phenomenon having reality only as a social institution. For this reason "Langue" is always and only contemporary to society with which it is identified.

Saussure defined language as simply the functioning of linguistic opposition, such opposition yield a pattern of relationship—the study of which constitutes linguistics.

Before beginning of the era of Bloomfield, Ferdinand de Saussure on the last of the nineteenth century and the first phase of twentieth century had defined the basic principles and philosophy of modern descriptive linguistics with his original interpretations and insightness. Saussure's influences upon subsequent linguistic theories has understandable been of a major importance. In the western world, at any case, all hues of structuralism have came under his influence. Actually, he had opened the first chapter of modern descriptive linguistics with his deep interpretations of the basic elements and philosophical aspects of linguistics. He had deeply influenced the coming generations of the scholars of science of languages who have recognized the time as "an Era of Saussure". Bloomfield has also praised the insight and original thinkings of Saussure.

Afterwards another linguistic movement that took its inspiration impart from Saussure's "course linguistique ge'ne'rale" is that which began with what is known either as "Prague school" or "Prague circle". The most influential person in this movement was Kikolass Trubetzkov (1890-1938) but professor Roman Jakobson (1896) had been the most responsible for extending Prague school theory practice into new areas of research.

In the last of the nineteenth century more attention had been drawn on "Phonomics". Really "Phonemics" is a science of unwritten languages to convert into a written form in which the substantial analysis of the sound of language has been dealt some significant sounds whether in vowels or consonants have been shortened out as phonems of the language. To trace out the phonems some sound symbols have been determined.

The founders of Prague school have established their

particular approach to study of language. They have explained "Phonology" as the study of the function of speech sounds and due to this emphasis they had also been recognized as "functionalist".

The basic method of the sound structuring of Prague school is entirely based upon contrast or opposition, for only by establishing differences as they believe is possible to construct a system of inter-relationships. As such, a phoneme may be defined as sum of these differentiating functioners. It is not a thing but an abstraction. Sounds in themselves are not phonemes, they are phonemes only in so far as they serve to distinguish meaning. Those sounds in a language which function phonemically, which significantly are determined simply by contrasting two sounds in identical environment. If this contrast is accompanied by a difference in meaning then the phonetic contrast is also Phonemic.

Professor Pike had also contributed two key volumes to this developing science of Linguistics—"Phonetics" and "Phonemics"—published after some interval, the first one in 1942 and the second in 1947. The outstanding features of "Phonetics" are most significant with precised description caught in articulatory terminology of many speech sounds that until then have generally escaped from the eyes of Phoneticians. In this book he also stressed the importance of environment as a factor influencing the pronounciation of sounds. His another book "*Phonemics*" has been widely used as a hand book of modern linguistics and accepted as "Eagle" of this science. It was recognised as a highly practical book with step-to-step directions for the purpose of day-to-day exercises, the chief value of this for reducing languages to writing.

The Phonetic method laid great stress on exact description of pronounciation and extensive use of I .P.A. phonetic symbols.

In this perspective Eugene A. Nida's "*Morphology : The Descriptive Analysis of Words*" was an excellent book, published in 1946 and its extensive revision in 1949. Eugene A. Nida was an executive secretary of the American Bible Society and also very active in the Summer Institute of Linguistics. During that period some other significant books have come up. Among them A. Gleason's "*Introduction to Descriptive Linguistics*", Archibald A. Hill's "*Introduction to linguistic structure*", Charls F. Hocket's "*A Course in Modern Linguistics*" and the most outstanding contribution to the linguistic world Zellig S. Harris's "*Structural Linguistics*" has given a sound impact on the entire world of science of languages defining the structural analysis and methods of languages. After fourteen years of the publication of the classic book of Bloomfield's "*Language*", the landmark book of Zellig S. Harris "*Structural Linguistics*" published in 1947 had open a new horizon of linguistic study. The outstanding publication of the new book of Harris has gained a wide scale momentum in the entire world of linguistic study. With the original thinking, deep insightness and model method of Harris, the modern descriptive linguistics has established as pure science which may be applied on all the languages of the world and its approaches and results would be universal and common to all. With this revolutionary contribution of Harris a new era of Linguistics has been started as the "Era of Structuralism". The critics of Harris and the scholars of linguistics has called it as "mathematics of linguistics".

Among the glaxy of significant scholars of Modern Linguistics, the names of Bernard Block, Henry Lee Smith, Jr. Morris, Swadesh, Charles C. Fries, Nelson Francis and George L. Trager, Martin Joos may also be included.

Afterwards, the most prominent and historical scholar of Structural Linguistics N. Chomsky has again deeply influenced and revolutionized the entire environment of linguistic science. Noam Chomsky had been one of the prominent students of Zellig Harris. Being an original philosopher and theoretician of linguistic science Chomsky has placed his new methods and principles of structuralism which has completely revolutionized and changed the whole atmosphere of linguistic world.

In 1964 N. Chomsky introduced his revolutionary principles

and new methods of Transformational and Generative grammar before the scholars and students of linguistics. At the same time, though, Halle has also published his famous article "Phonology in Generative Grammar" and after four years in 1968. N. Chomsky and Halley have jointly published their landmark excellent book "Generative Phonology and Sound Pattern of English", which gave a revolutionary impact on the whole world of linguistic study. Chomsky has defined and established that Kernel Sentences are the last forms of the phrase construction. According to Chomsky Kernel sentences are the basic sentences of a language. He has proved that there are not more than five to seven Kernel sentences in almost all the languages of the world. With this the scientific and model approach, as well as the original principles of Chomsky many scholars, professors and students have come up in Hindi also. Some of them may be mentioned here. In this respect Ramesh Chandra Mahrotra and Chitranjan Ker have published a book "*Hindi Ka Naveentam Vyakaran*" in 1986 which has attracted the attention of the scholars and students of linguistics. In this context, it may also be referred here that the revolutionary book of Chomsky, "*The Aspect of Principals of Sentence Construction*" has been translated in Hindi by Ramanath Sahay and published in 1975 by Rajasthan Hindi Granth Academy, Jaipur.

In the field of Phonemics, in 1973, David Stampe has pointed out some defects of Generative Phonology in a research paper "Dessertation on Natural Phonology". After three years Knokke Hiest has introduced his new theory "Kankreet Phonology" and he has elaborately defined his generative Phonology. In the same year Daniel Dinsen has presented his principles of Atomic Phonology and interpreted it in an article "Some preliminaries to Atomic Phonology". In this way, after the new principles of Generative Phonology of Chomsky, there were three kinds of theories which have appeared in the last phase of twenteeth century, but on these new theories no work has yet been observed in Hindi by the author.

In this context, an excellent example of scientific achievements of structural linguistics, may be referred here. When our ex-Foreign Minister Shri Atal Bihari Bajpayi in 1977 had expressed his desire to deliver his speech in our national language Hindi. To implement the wishes of India so many problems and complications had aroused before U.N.O. To recognition of a language in U.N.O. may be a political matter, but from the liuguistic point of view, that was a very complicated matter. Hindi is not a recognized language in U.N.O.

To solve the linguistic problems of U.N.O. Noam Chomsky, the most prominent and leading linguist of America, was invited. Actually there were so many complicated problems before the U.N.O. to convert the speech of Hindi of our Foreign Minister in all the recognized languages of the U.N.O., so that the speech of Hindi may be listened and perceived in their own national languages of the representatives of U.N.O. To solve this most complicated linguistic, phonetic and phonemic problems, Noam Chomsky applied his scientific principles and methods and devices of structural linguistics.

Undoubtedly, it was a landmark success and wonderful achievement of structural linguistics. From this example it has already been proved that now, the modern linguistics has already been converted as a pure science and the results of it are universal and common to all.

In the first half of the nineteenth century historical and comparative study of langugages got momentum and several scholars had led the way. In this perspective some important scholars might be mentioned here.

Though Sir William Jones was not a professional philologist he had studied Sanskrit with keen interest. He was educated in law and served as a jurist on the bench of the British Court of Calcutta from 1783 till his death. Generally it has been accepted that the beginning of the Comparative Linguistics from his statement, contained in a speech, was delivered before the Asiatic Society on the 2nd February, 1786:

> "The Sanscrit language, whatever be its antiquity, is of a wonderful structure; more perfect than the Greek, more copious than the Latin, and more exquisitely refined than either, yet bearing to both of them a stronger affinity, both in the roots of verbs and in the forms of grammar, than could possibly have been produced by accident; so strong indeed, that no philologer could examine them all three, without believing them to have sprung from same common source, which, perhaps, no longer exists (italics mine): there is a similar reason, though not quite so forcible, for supposing that both the Gothick and the Celtick, though blended with a very different idiom, had the same origin with the Sanscrit; and the old Persian might be added to the same family."

Some scholars came to realise the similarity of these languages, even before Jones, but no one prior to him, had reached the conclusion, that these similarties must be due to a common descent from hypothetical earlier language. Rasmus Kristian Rask (1787 to 1832) a Dane Scholar had cleared the way of comparative linguistics presenting the aims and methods of comparative linguistics. A German Jocob Grimm had published a detail comparative Grammar of all the Germanic languages and he elaborated upon Rosk's largely correct but limited information. He may be regarded the father of Comparative Linguistics but his great debt to Rusmus Kristian Rask is enourmous. Grimm was able to set up a series of formula like statements which was later on called "Laws". Grimm's law whatever amounts to considerably more than a set up of phonetic relations concerning Germanic to Indo-European family of languages.

Franz Bopp (1791 to 1867), in this connection, had played a significant role and his comparative grammar of Sanskrit, Zend, Greek, Latin, Lithuanian, Gothea and German. The main emphasis of Bopp had laid down on morphology. He deffered radically from Rask and Grimm, both of them were interested mainly with phonetic change. Bopp was Sanskritish by training and method of words analysis he used are those by means of which a Sanskrit "word" is resolved into its parts.

Though, Yakob Grimm (1785 to 1863) was a son of a pleader and he studied law at first uptill the period, the study of ancient languages has been accepted as most significant and small languages were also important with the eye of science of linguistics. In 1819 he has published a grammar of German language and then he became a professor in Burline for teaching Linguistics.

Franz Bopp has come Paris and studied the eastern languages having a goal of studying Sanskrit. In 1861 his book was published on the methods and rules of comparative study of languages. In his book he has established the comparative study of Sanskrit with Greek, Latin, Irani and German languages.

Upto 1870 Linguistics had achieved great importance, so that Maxmullar, Whitne etc. have felt prouad.

Basically sounds are the subjects of Physics but such sounds which are recognized in Physics may be heard and even not be heard. But in linguistics the forms of sounds are not very extensive. In language our purpose is very limited only for those sounds which are used in languages and which are arculated by the human organs of speech.

At first the centre of study of linguistics established in Germany. After that it has been shifted to Paris. But lastly America has become the main centre of the developing science of Modern linguistics. The main emphasis, in Modern linguistics has been given on the present speaking form of language, rather than historical forms of a living language has been finally interpreted than historical and comparative study. In Paris the Historical and Comparative study of the languages has been declared as out of the context of modern linguistics. In this respect, Maharshi Pāṇini has been again remembered here, who had accepted the living speaking forms of his contemporary Sanskrit in his "*Ashtadhyayi*". It may also be recalled here that India for the first time had presented to European eyes a complete and accurate description of a language which was not based upon theory but upon observation and face-to-face interview of informant of the original speaker of a language.

In the mean time some other specific branches of linguistics have also been developed as "Tonetics" (Īntonation), Meta Linguistics, Dialectology and Linguistic Geography, but Meta Linguistics was not directly concerned with Linguistics. In this field a most significant book of Kaneth Pike has been published "Intonation of American English." Among the prominent scholars of Phonetics and Phonemics the name if scripture Daniel Jones must be specially mentioned here. The first edition of his masterpiece book "*An Outline of English Phonetics*" had been published in 1918 and its nineteenth edition had come up in 1962 and after that several editions of this very famous book have been published. In the first phase of twentieth century the most prominent book of Daniel Jones, actually has laid down the foundation of scientific study of Phonetics of several languages of the world. More than a dozen books of Daniel Jones on different aspect of English pronunciation have been published. Among them some prominent books may be mentioned here:- *"An English Pronouncing Dictionary"*, "The *Phoneme* : its nature and use", "The Pronunciation of English", "The Problem of a National Script for India", "Cordinal Vowels" including some Gramophone records (spoken by Daniel Jones) and Lingua Phone records with explanatory Booklets etc.

In this connection, one of the famous Phoneticians of British school, Firth had also paved the way of a new trends of Phonetics and his separate school on the name of "Prosodic" had been started near about 1948 in London. The first and the last scholars of Firth School was Dr. Vishwa Nath Prasad, who had worked on *"Phonetics and Phonological Study of Bhojpuri"* in 1950 under the guidance of Firth. But due to the early death of Firth his school could not be survived.

As a matter of fact, in western world, the detailed and deep study of the sounds of languages got momentum from the second half of nineteenth century with the establishment of "International Phonetic Association", London in which each and every languages of the world might be transcribed. In this respect Daniel Jones, the great phonetician of Britain had taken a lead. He had studied so many languages of the world and transcribed them in I.P.A. The American linguistics were also agreed with Daniel Jones. He had also tape-recorded several languages as the raw materials of their descriptive analysis.

On the basis of the principles and methods of Daniel Jones in 1958, Golok Bihari Dhal has published his book in Hindi "*Dhwani Vigyan*" from Bihar Hindi Granth Academy, Patna providing detailed analysis of Phonetics with minute observations. Though, Golok Bihari Dhal belonged to Orissa, but he was a well trained Phonetician of London School. His book has been well popularized and its several editions being published.

In the background of the excellent achievement of Modern Descriptive Linguistics, many scholars and students have deeply influenced and inspired also in India and they have contributed several Doctorate theses, research papers and articles in the Hindi also. Some of them may be referred here. In this field Dr. Bhola Nath Tiwari has collected some significant articles in his book "*Hindi Bhasha Ki Dhwani Sanrachna*" published in 1981. They may be underlined here:

"Hindi Dhwaniyon ka adhyan : Ek sarvekchhan"—Dr. Bhola Nath Tiwari, "Hindi ki Swar Vaiwastha"—Dr. Sharda Bhasin, "Aksharant"—Dr. Kailash Chandra Bhatia, "Hindi Ke Swar Swanimo ke Prabhedak Abhilakshan"—Dr. Sharda Bhasin, "Hindi ke Vainjan swanimo ke Prabhedak abhilakshan"— Dr. Ramesh Chandra Garg, "Hindi ke 'h'dhwanigram ki dhwanatmak Prakriti"—Dr. Ravindra Nath Shrivastava, "yah", "bah" ka uchcharan aur 'h' sambandhi kuchh samasyayen" —Dr. Kuiba Doi, "Bharat ki Bhashayon me Mahapraṇ Vyanjan"—Dr. William Bright, "Hindi ki Mahapraṇ Dhwaniyon me saral Vainjan ya Samyukta Vainjan"—Dr. Bhola Nath Tiwari, "Hindi me/mh/ke swanimiye ster per ek Tippṇi"—Dr. Lakshmi Narayan Mittal, "Hindi me Nasikya Anuswar Aur Anunasikta ki samasya"—Dr. Ravindra Nath Shrivastava, "Hindi me Anunasikta"—Tej Narayan Bhatiya, "Hindi ka Aksharik Vivechan"—Dr. Murari Lal Upreti, "Hindi me Akshar Sanrachna"—Dr. Ramesh Chandra Mahrotra, "Hindi me Balaghat"—Dr. Bhola Nath Tiwari, "Hindi me Shabda Balaghat"—Dr. R.C. Gupta, "Hindi Anutan"—Dr. Bhola Nath Tiwari, "Bhasha ka Ragatmak Tatwa Tatha "Y" aur "W" ka Ragatmak Nirupan"—Dr. Vishwa Nath Prasad, "Hindi ki Arthyukta Bhashetar Dhwaniyan"—Dr. Ramesh Chandra Mahrotra, "Manak Hindi ke Alpgyat Swan"—Dr. Ramesh Chandra Mahrotra, "Swaraghat"—Acharya Kamta Prasad 'Guru', "Sandhi"—Kellog, "Varna Sandhiyan"—Dr. Acharya Kishori Das Vajpayee, "Vivirti"—Dr. Mahaveer Saran Jain, "Hindi me Sanghita"—Dr. Kripa Shankar Singh, "Hindi me Nayi Dhwaniyan tatha Unke Liye Naya Chinha"—Dr. Dhirendra Verma, "Hindi Swaraghat"—Dr. Dhirendra Verma. During that period an important article may also be underlined here—"Sandhyaksharo ka Apurna Uchcharan"—Prof. Guru Prasad.

Apart from these articles, some other remarkable research papers have also been come out—"Re-Construction of Pali Phonology in South-East Asia"—Dr. Saryoo Prasad, "Magahi ke Udgam srot"—Dr. Saryoo Prasad.

In the background of the excellent achievement of Modern Descriptive Linguistics many scholars and student have been deeply influenced and inspired in India also and they have contributed some significant Doctorate theses and books also. Some of them might be quoted here as in:

"Hindi Dhwani aur Dhwaniki"—Dr. Ramesh Chandra Mahrotra, "Hindi Bhasha me Akshar tatha Shabda Seema"—

Dr. Kailash Chandra Bhatia, "Magahi Dhwani tatha Vertani"—Dr. Saryoo Prasad, "Hindi Dhwaniyan aur Unka Uchcharan"—Dr. Bhola Nath Tiwari, "Pranisthit Dhwanigramic Adhyan"—Dr. Mahavir Saran Jain, "Hindi me Sandhi"—Lakshmi Narayan Mittal, "Samkaleen Hindi Roop Swanim Vigyan"—Sudhakar Singh, "Hindi ke Adi Vyanjan Guchhon ki Prakirti aur Vitran with special reference to Russian Language"—Dr. Ravindra Nath Shrivastava, "A study of Hindi Intonation"—Raplimoor and "Hindi Phonology : A study of the treatment of Indo-Aryan vowel sequences"—Norihika Uchida (1977). In the continuation of the above outstanding publications some other books may also be underlined as follows : "Topics in Hindi-Urdu Phonology"—Manjari Ohala, "The contrastive study of Hindi and Japanese word Phonology"—Sharda Bhasin, "A Descriptive study of Magahi Phonology"—Dr. Saryoo Prasad.

Some more articles have also been published on the new trends of "Generative Phonology" of Chomsky by Narang and Baker, Manjari Ohala, Tej Krishna Bhatiya, Sharda Jaggi, Ramesh Chandra Garg, Ravindra Nath Shrivastva and Sharda Bhasin. In this perspective an important book of Hindi Grammar under title "*Hindi ka Naveentam Veej Vyakran*" written by Dr. Ramesh Chandra Mahrotra and Dr. Chitranjanker, both are from the Department of Linguistics, Ravi Shankar University, M.P., published in 1986. This has been written on the basic principles of N. Chomsky, who had established a new method of structuralism.

It is quite evident from the above references and the significant works that India has also achieved remarkable success in the different fields of Linguistics, specially in Phonetics and Phonology. In any case, India has not left behind in the progress of Modern Descriptive Linguistics.

In the beginning of the modern age Ramkrishna Gopal Bhandarkar had taken a lead and could be able to arrange Wilson Lectures in 1877. Though, Bhandarker had preserved the traditions of India, but he had also studied the theories and methods of European scholars. During that time some European scholars had also undertaken the study of Indian languages. Of them Trump for Sindhi, Kodwell for Drabedian and for the comparative study of Indo-Aryan languages. Brimz and Harnel-a-ye were the prominent linguists who had showed their profound interest in the study of Indian languages. One of the great Linguists of India Jorge Abraham Griarson had conducted a wide scale Linguistic Survey of India in several volumes with his great zeal and endless enthuism, which has been recognized as an excellent work on Indian Languages. But his methods of survey were defective and not upto the mark. In this field Turner and Zeul Block have presented a comparative and historical study of Indian languages. The Nepali Dictionary of Turner and Development of Marathi and Indo-Aryan languages of Block were the unique books. Dr. S.K. Chatterjee, one of the prominent linguists of India, will be always remembered with great respect due to his historical book "*Origin and Development of Bengali Language*" which was regarded as "Encyclopaedia of Indian Languages". He was not merely a linguist, but also a well-known scholar of ancient history and culture. He was one of the best orators of English. Besides this, he had been the chairman of the West Bengal Legislative Council for a considerable period. Keeping in view the scholarship of Dr. S.K. Chatterjee in the field of historical and comparative linguistics and public services, the most prestigious award of India "Padmshri" has been confirred on him by the Honourable President of India.

In this regard Dr. Siddheshwar Verma has also contributed his valuable work to Indian Phonetics and he had searched out the languages of Dardi along with its dialects. In this respect, some significant linguists of India have also established themselves with their outstanding books on different languages. Among such brilliant linguists, some are Dr. S.M. Katre (Konkani), Dr. Dhirendra Verma (Brajbhasha), Banarasi Das Jain (Punjabi), Vanikant Kakoti (Assamia), Babu Ram Saksena (Awadhi), Dr. Vishwa Nath Prasad and Dr. Udya Narayan Tiwari both are on (Bhojpuri), Ramasyami Aiyar (Dravidian) and Dr. Herdeo Bahri (Lahndi). But all these works are mainly based on historical linguistics, not on modern descriptive linguistics. One of the most brilliant and prominent linguists of India, the name of Dr. A.M. Ghatage, Ex. Head of the Department of Linguistics, Deccan College of Post-Graduate and Research Institute, Poona University must be remembered with great honour who had controlled Historical and Comparative Philology and at the same time Modern Descriptive Linguistics also with his profound knowledge and deep study. Among other Prakrit scholars Dr. P.L. Vaidya and Dr. Hira Lal Jain were also very famous. In this field, Dr. Sukumar Sen, Ex. of the Department of Linguistics, Calcutta University had also published his important book on *Historical and Comparative Study of Prakrit Languages*.

Several years ago, though Linguistic Society of India had been started from Lahore but after the sad demise of Bulner, the Institution became laxed and its office had been shifted from Lahore to Calcutta. In Calcutta it had gained momentum but when the famous Rock Feller Foundation of America had planned to extend one of the most prominent and developing science of linguistics, Dr. S.M. Katry, Ex. Director of Deccan College Post-Graduate and Research Institute, Poona University had decided to organize summer school of Linguistics in India also with the help of Rock Feller Foundation of America. Several famous scholars of America and India of Modern Linguistics had been invited in Deccan College, Pune to attend their classes. On the invitation, some leading linguists of the world had also come up in these summer schools to take their classes. It had continued for more than five years in different places of India and during that period more than one thousand professors, research scholars, students and educationist of other fields have attended their classes and had gone under training which was essential for Modern Linguistics. They had spread out the modern science of Linguistics all over India. And, as a result some universities of South and North India have opened their separate departments of Linguistics. In Calcutta University, one of the oldest universities of India, had been established long before a chair of Linguistics and had opened the Department of Science of Languages.

But particularly in North India, it could not got warm response and as such, a few Universities of North India could be enable to open their departments of Linguistics. Due to the poor response the students of North India had suffered a lot and they are still unknown with the great achievements of this developing science of Linguistics, which is, exactly a matter of grave concern. Apart from this, the syllabies of the Departments. of all Language and Literature of the post graduate master degrees are still based on a very old pattern and as such, the old and unfreshed materials are presented to the students, which is a serious matter on which the urgent attention of Human Resource Development Department of Government of India as well as the State Governments must be drawn with immediate effect and separate Department of Linguistics must be opened in all the Universities of India without further delay.

NOTES

1. Language — Leonard Bloomfield, Reprinted by Motilal Banarsi Dass, 1963, pp. 10-12.
2. Language — XXV, 1992.
3. Ibid.

2
INVENTORY OF PHONEMES

Number of Phonemes

In all there are fifty-three phonemes in Magahī. Of these forty-five are segmental phonemes and eight are supra-segmental phonemes which are classified as below :

Segmental Phonemes

Vowels

Pure Vowels :			Diphthongs :	
/i		u	/ə͜i	ə͜u
I		U	a͜i	a͜u
e	ə	o	o͜i	e͜u
		a/	u͜i	i͜u/

Consonants

/p	t	ṭ	c	k
ph	th	ṭh	ch	kh
b	d	ḍ	j	g
bh	dh	ḍh	jh	gh
	s			h
m	n			
	l			
	r	ṛ		
w			y/	

Supra-Segmental Phonemes

Nasalization /˜/
Juncture / + /
Intonation Phonemes :
Pitch Levels /1 2 3 4/
Terminal Contours /↓↑/

Section I

SEGMENTAL PHONEMES

3
VOWELS

Pure Vowels

Phonological Structure

There are eight pure vowel phonemes in Magahī.[1] The phonemic structure of the vowels shows two ways contrast which depends upon tongue height and tongue position. There is four-fold contrast in tongue height as (i) high, (ii) lower high, (iii) mid and (iv) low, and three-fold contrast in tongue position as (i) front, (ii) central and (iii) back. The lip-position is predictable. Almost all the rounded vowels are restricted to the back part of the tongue, as the unrounded vowels are confined to the rest parts except the back low vowel.

Diphthongs

There exist eight diphthong phonemes which have a falling quality. Out of them /ə͜i a͜i o͜i/ and / u͜i / end with a front vowel and /ə͜u a͜u e͜u/ and /i͜u/ end with a back vowel. Their detailed analysis is given in the chapter on diphthongs.

Nasalization in Vowels

Any vowel can be nasalized which distinguishes it from the oral vowel. *e.g.*,

/sajh/	'honest'	/sãjh/	'evening'
/bhag/	'fly away'	/bhãg/	'an intoxicating herb'
/oṭ/	'vote'	/õṭ/	'side'

Nasalization is phonemic in Magahī (chap.4).

Classification of Vowels

Phonetically on the basis of duration these vowels may be grouped into two classes : (i) short, and (ii) long.

Short and Long

Short vowels consist of three /I U ə/ and long vowels are five /i e a o u/.

Vowel-Contrast

The contrast between the vowels can be illustrated with following examples :

Contrast between Short Vowels

/I U ə/

Initial contrast

/Inar/ 'well' /Unar/ 'open' /ənar/ 'pomegranate'

Medial contrast

/ghIr/ 'to be surrounded' /ghUr/ 'turn back'
/ghər/ 'house'

Final contrast

/bəhI/ 'account book' /bəhU/ 'daughter-in-law'
/bəhə/ 'please flow'

Contrast between Long Vowels

/i e a o u/

Initial contrast

/i a o u/

/ĩṭ/ 'brick' /ãṭ/ 'a bundle of hay'

/õṭ/	'side'	/ũṭ/	'camel'
	/e o/		
/enhĩ/	'here'	/onhĩ/	'there'
	/a o/		
/al/	'came'	/ol/	'tuber'(a tuber eaten as a vegetable.)

Medial contrast

/i e a o u/

/sir/	'head'	/ser/	'lion or a measurement'
/sar/	'substance'	/sor/	'sources of water'
/sur/	'blind or melody'		

Final contrast

/i e a o u/

/Pari/	'turn'	/Pare/	'on the other side of river'
/Para/	'murcury'	/Paro/	'a popular name for girls'
/bala/	'golden bracelet'	/balu/	'sand'

Contrast between Long and Short Vowels

/i I u U ə a/

Initial Contrast

/ə a/

/ əb/	'now'	/ab/	'faith'
/ən/	'grain'	/an/	'next day or dignity'

Medial Contrast

/I i/

/bIn/	'without'	/bin/	'a musical instrument'
/cIta/	'funeral pyre'	/cita/	'tiger'
/lIkh/	'write'	/likh	'an insect of hair', 'louse'

/U u/

/mUr/	'turn'	/mur/	'capital'
/kUṭ/	'a sort of sound for cutting'	/kuṭ/	'press'
/sUt/	'sleep'	/sut/	'thread'

/ə a/

/bəs/	'stop'	/bas/	'house'
/nəg/	'costly stone'	/nag/	'a cobra'
/hər/	'plough'	/har/	'defeat or garland'
/jəl/	'burn'	/jal/	'net'

/I/ /e a o u/

/mIl/	'meet'	/mel/	'similarity'
/mal/	'goods'	/mol/	'cost'
/mul/	'root'		

/U/ /i e a o u/

/sUt/	'sleep'	/sit/	'dew'
/sẽt/	'preserve'	/sat/	'seven'
/sot/	'sources of water'	/sut/	'thread'

/ə/ /i e a o u/

/mər/	'die'	/mir/	'the first one'
/mer/	'a set'	/mar/	'beating'
/mor/	'peacock'	/mur/	'capital'

Final contrast

/ə a/

/hərə/	'please take up'	/həra/	'green'
/bələ/	'please burn'	/bəla/	'trouble'
/jərə/	'please burn'	/jəra/	'some what'

Length

Neglecting the difference in the qualities of vowels and bringing the contrast on the feature of length we can fit these eight phonemes as follows :

i	i:	u	u:
	e:		o:
	a		a:

Further, we can set length as a separate phoneme and write the vowels as :

i	u	
e	o	+ :
	a	

Thus, we might sum up six basic vowel phonemes on the whole.

But this is not considered feasible here owing to the following reasons :

1. The distinction between long and short vowels does not depend upon length only but they are distinctive

due to their tongue height and position, *i.e.,* if the long /i/ and /u/ are high, the short /I/ and /U/ are lower high. On the other hand the short /ə/ is central and mid, the long /a/ is back and low. The /I ə U/ and /i a u/ are as different as the remaining vowels are contrastive to each other.

2. The language does not present symmetry between long and short vowels, *i.e.,* there are only three short vowels whereas five long vowels exist.
3. The allophonic variations of these vowels show apparently that length is not distinctive in the dialect, *i.e.,* finally all long vowels have their relatively short (half-long) forms. On the other hand, the short mid vowel /ə/ occurs finally as a relatively long (half-long) form. *e.g.,*

(a)	I	[dho·bi·]	/dhobi/	'washerman'
	II	[ja·re·]	/jare/	'to be burnt'
	III	[o·jha·]	/ojha/	'a superstitious man'
	IV	[ka·bu·]	/kabu/	'strength'
	V	[ə˃gho·]	/əgho/	'to be fully satisfied'
(b)		[Uṭhə^̣]	/Uṭhə/	'please get up'
		[k˂əh̄ə^̣]	/kəhə/	'please tell'

4. Even in the sequence of vowels length is not significant. Length is an over-lapping phenomenon in the vowel-sequences. It is obvious in the following examples :

/Pie/	'let him drink'
/PIe/	'let him drink'
/jua/	'gamble'
/jUa/	'gamble'

etc.

General Remarks

The following general statement can be made :

1. Phonetically all Magahī vowels lean towards the centre, *i.e.*, front vowels like behind the cardinal front position and back vowels are more forward than the cardinals, except the central vowel which tends to be back.
2. Phonemically every vowel occurs initially, medially as well as finally.
3. All the vowels are voiced and syllabic, however /i/ and /u/ might be observed as non-syllabic also. Phonetically the second element of the diphthongs is non-syllabic, *i.e.*, *e.g.*, [əi̯], [au̯] etc.
4. Broadly speaking, although all vowels have been divided as short and long, the allophonic variations of the vowels show one more quality *i.e.*, half long. The duration of the vowels, therefore, can be discriminated into three types : (i) long, (ii) half long and (iii) short. The long and half long varieties of the long vowels occur in mutually exclusive environments whereas the half long quality of short vowel /ə/ occurs only finally. The short quality occurs along with short vowels, *e.g.*,

    (i) The long quality occurs usually in close syllables only with long vowels, *e.g.*,

[likh]	/likh/	'louse'
[sut]	/sut/	'thread'
[bəsul]	/bəsul/	'paid'
[Pəror]	/pəror/	'a kind of vegetable', 'vegetable marrow'

    (ii) The half long quality occurs in open syllables with long and short vowels, *e.g.*,

[pi·]	/pi/	'drink'
[kha·]	/kha/	'eat'
[te·li·]	/teli/	'oilman'
[sa·h̄u·]	/sahu/	'a surname'
[Ih̄o·ra·]	/Ihora/	'request'
[əbe·ra·]	/əbera/	'clear weather'
[tha·li·]	/thali/	'plate'
[Uṭhə^·]	/Uṭhə/	'please get up'
[bəiṭhə]	/bəiṭhə/	'please sit down'

(iii) The short quality occurs only with short vowels, *e.g.*,

[Ĩjo·rIya·]	/ĨjorIya/	'moonlight'
[gh<Iya·h̄I]	/ghIyahI/	'what is made with ghee'
[ənk<ər]	/ənkər/	'of another'

ALLOPHONICS

Allophonic Characteristics of Vowels

The allophonic character of Magahī vowels can be stated in three groups which are as under :

Short Vowels : Group 1

Those short vowels which have only one allophone. These are /I/ and /U/.

Short Vowels : Group 2

Another short vowel /ə/ has three allophones.

Long Vowels : Group 3

Every long vowel has two sorts of allophones. These are /i e a o/ and /u/ which never occur finally as their long forms. Their detailed description is given below.

Descriptions and Distributions of Vowels

Group 1

I / I/ is front lower high unrounded short vowel occuring initially, medially as well as finally. It has only one allophone. *e.g.*,

[I]	[Ink<ər]	/Inkər/	'his'
[Iyar]	/Iyar/	'friend', 'familiar'	
[phIk'ka·]	/phIkka/	'tasteless'	
[dIk]	/dIk/	'disturbance'	
[pa·rI]	/parI/	'chance', 'turn'	
[jUa·nI]	/jUanI/	'youth'	

II. /U/ is back lower high rounded short vowel. It also has only one allophone and occurs initially, medially and finally , *e.g.*,

[U]	[Uta/h̄Ul]	/UtahUl/	'hurry'
[Ura·h̄əl]	/Urahəl/	'overhauled'	
[həsUli.]	/həsUli]	'an ornament worn on neck'	
[cərUa·]	/cərUa/	'water's pot'	
[k<əh̄U]	/kəhU/	'please tell'	
[bo·kU]	/bokU/	'fool'	

Group 2

III. /ə/ is mid unrounded central short vowel. It is slightly retracted to back. There are three allophones as under :

[ə>] a short form which is more retracted to back followed by velar stops. It occurs initially as well as medially. *e.g.*,

[ə>ga·ṛi·]	/əgaṛi/	'forward'
[ə>kh<əro·ṭ]	/əkhəroṭ/	'a dry fruit', 'walnut'

[mə˃k‿'kh˂ən]	/məkkhən/	'butter'
[pə˃gha·]	/pəgha/	'rope'

[ə·^] a slightly rising and half long form occurs only in final position. *e.g.*,

[Uṭhə·^]	[Uṭhə/	'please get up'
[b͜əiṭhə·^]	/b͜əiṭhə/	'please sit down'
[k͜ha·lə·^]	/khalə/	'please eat'
[a·bə·^]	/abə/	'Please come on'

[ə] a higher low short form occuring elsewhere. *e.g.*,

[əc‿·chət]	/əcchət/	'grains of white unbroken rice used on religious occasions'
[ədəra·]	/ədəra/	'a fortnight of rainy season'
[bəsəl]	/bəsəl/	'established'
[ləc‿chən]	/ləcchən/	'feature'

Group 3

IV. /i/ is front high unrounded long vowel. It is slightly higher than its corresponding /I/. It has two allophones which are as under :

[i] a high long quality occuring initially and medially in mono-syllabic and disyllabic words of closed syllables. *e.g.*,

[ĩṭ]	/ ĩṭ/	'brick'
[id]	/id/	'a Muslim festival'
[bin]	/bin/	'a musical instrument'
[kh˂ir]	/khir/	'pudding of rice and milk'
[sərir]	/sərir]	'body'

[i·] a half long form occuring elsewhere. It does not occur initially. *e.g.*,

[ko'ta'hi']	/kotahi/	'miserliness'
[ba·ki·]	/baki/	'credit', 'dues'
[bəṛhi·]	/bəṛhi/	'carpenter'
[dho· bi·]	/dhobi/	'washerman'
[si.ṛhi·]	/siṛhi/	'stair case'
[kh<əmi·ra·]	/khəmira/	'seasoned', 'yeast'

V. /e/ is front mid unrounded long vowel. It has two allophones which are given below :

[e] a long form occurs initially as well as medially in monosyllabic and disyllabic words of closed syllable. *e.g.*,

[ek]	/ek/	'one'
[ẽṛ]	/ẽṛ/	'heel'
[kh<et]	/khet/	'field'
[tel]	/tel/	'oil'
[səhēj]	/səhej/	'preserve'
[bəṛẽṛ]	/bəṛẽṛ/	'wooden ceiling'

[e·] a half long quality occuring elsewhere. *e.g.*,

[e·j'ja.]	/ejja/	'here'
[e·k<əisa·]	/ekəisa/	'a day of twenty one'
[ne·ba·ri]	/nebari/	'hay'
[se·nUria.]	/senUria/	'reddish'
[pəire·]	/pəire/	'swim'
[məre·]	/məre/	'die'

VI. /a/ is back low unrounded long vowel. It has the usual two allophones as follows :

[a] a long quality occuring in monosyllabic and disyllabic words of closed syllable initially and medially only. *e.g.*,

[ãm/	/ãm/	'mango'
[as]	/as/	'hope'
[jat/	/jat/	'caste'
[sas]	/sas/	'mother-in-law'
[məlal]	/məlal/	'complain'
[sIyar]	/sIyar/	'Jackal'

[a·] a half long quality occuring elsewhere. *e.g.*,

[ã·ṭi.]	/ãṭi/	''a bundle of straw'
[ã·dhi·]	/ãdhi/	'storm'
[tha·li·]	/thali/	'plate'
[dIya·ra·]	/dIyara/	'sandy land within a river'
[əbha·ga·]	/əbhaga/	'unfortunate'
[pənso·k͜'kha.]	/pənsokkha/	'rainbow'

VII. /o/ is back mid rounded long vowel. There are the usual two allophones as follows :

[o] a long quality occuring initially and medially in monosyllabic and disyllabic words in closed syllable. *e.g.*,

[ol]	/ol/	'tuber'
[or]	/or/	'the last point'
[jhõk]	/jhõk/	'speed'
[cobh]	/cobh/	'suck'

[pəror]	/pəror/	'a sort of vegetable'
[k<əlol]	/kəlol/	'play with water'

[o·] a half long form occuring elsewhere, *e.g.*,

[o·jha·]	/ojha/	'a superstitious man'
[o·h̄a·ri·]	/ohari/	'the fore part of roof through which water falls'
[ə>gho·ri·]	/əghori/	'dirty man', 'tantrik sadhu'
[jIno·ra·]	/jInora/	'a kind of grain'
[ə>gho·]	/əgho/	'to be fully satisfied'
[ə͜i̯bo·]	/ə͜ibo/	'could I come?'

VIII. /u/ is back high rounded long vowel. It has also the two allophones like /i/. They are as in :

[u] a high long quality occuring initially and medially in monosyllabic and disyllabic words of closed syllable, *e.g.*,

[ũn]	/ũn/	'wool'
[ub]	/ub/	'vex'
[sut]	/sut/	'thread'
[cũn]	/cũn/	'twisted cloth'
[bəbul]	/bəbul/	'gum tree'
[səh̄ur]	/səhur/	'tact'

[u·] a half long form occuring elsewhere. It does not occur initially, *e.g.*,

[ka·bu·]	/kabu/	'strength'
[ga·rũ·]	/garũ/	'squeeze'

[ma·nu·]	/manu/	'would I accept?'
[ba·bu·]	/babu/	'father or master'
[cu·ṛi·]	/cuṛi/	'bracelet'
[chu·ra·]	/chura/	'dagger'

Diphthongs

Introductory

A diphthong is an 'independent vowel glide'[1] in which the tongue starts in the position of one vowel and immediately leaves it to glide towards another vowel without any obstruction of the air current. It is a combination of a syllabic and a non-syllabic vowel.

Classification of Diphthongs

On the basis of the direction of tongue motion the eight diphthong phonemes of Magahī can be grouped into two parts :

Having (a) front off-glide and
(b) back off-glide

(a) which tends to be front /ə͜i a͜i o͜i u͜i/ and
(b) which tends to be back /ə͜u a͜u e͜u i͜u/.

All the diphthongs are falling *i.e.*, the first vowel of these diphthongs is more sonorous than the second one.

Diphthongs and Nasalization

These diphthongs also show a distinction against their nasalized counter parts, *e.g.*,

/bha͜i/	'brother'	/bha͜ĩ/	'a fearful sound'
/cha͜u/	'acting'	/cha͜ũ/	'shade'

/so͜i/	'sources of water	/so͜ĩ/	'a sort of sound'
/ka͜i/	'mass'	/kã͜i/	'a sort of noise'

In a few cases nasalized and non-nasalized diphthongs occur in free variation also. Examples follow :

/ə͜ura/	'myrobalan'	/ə̃͜ura/	'myrobalan'
/ə͜ukha/	'a supersti-tious per-formance	/ə̃͜ukha/	'a superstitious performance'
/ke͜uṛa/	'orange'	/kẽ͜uṛa/	'orange'

Contrast

These diphthongs show their contrast as follows :

(a) diphthong Vs. Diphthong and

(b) Diphthong Vs. Vowel.

The contrast can be illustrated with the following examples :

Contrast between Diphthongs

/ ə͜i a͜i o͜i u͜i /

/jə͜i/	'victory'	/ja͜i/	'he may go'
/so͜i/	'sources of water'	/su͜i/	'needle'

/ə͜u/, /a͜u/, /i͜u/, /e͜u/

/sə͜u/	'hundred'	/sa͜u/	'a surname', 'sahu or sau'
/si͜u/	'Lord Śiva'	/se͜u/	'apple'

/ə͜i ə͜u a͜i a͜u o͜i e͜u u͜i i͜u/

/nə͜i/	'no'	/nə͜u/	'nine'
/ga͜i/	'cow'	/ga͜u/	'sing'

/so͜i/	'sources of water'	/se͜u/	'apple'
/su͜i/	'needle'	/si͜u/	'Lord Śiva'

Contrast between Diphthongs and Pure Vowels

1. /ə͜i/, /ə/

/ə͜ib/	'demerites'	/əb/	'now'
/kə͜il/	'done'	/kəl/	'tomorrow'

/ə͜i/, /i/

/pə͜i/	'charge/	/pi/	'drink'
/cə͜it/	'a month of spring	/cit/	'lay down on back'

/ə͜i/, /e/

/mə͜il/	'dirt'	/mel/	'similarity'
/jə͜i/	'victory'	/je/	'any one'

2. /a͜i/, /a/

/ga͜i/	'cow'	/ga/	'sing'
/ba͜il/	'outsider'	/bal/	'hair'

/a͜i/, /i/

/ba͜il/	'outsider'	/bil/	'hole'
/ka͜i/	'moss'	/ki/	'what?'

3. /o͜i/, /o/

/to͜i/	'lace'	/to/	'then'

/o͜i/, /i/

/ko͜i/	'any one'	/ki/	'what?'
/po͜iya/	'a kind of vegetable/	/piya/	'lover or husband'

4. /u͜i/, /u/

/bu͜ia/	'a subject of fear'	/bua/	'father's sister'
/bu͜i/	'a subject of fear'	/bu/	'smail'

/u͜i/, /i/

/su͜ia/	'needle'	/sia/	'Sītā'

5. /i͜u/, /i/

/ji͜uwa/	'creature'	/jia/	'heart'
/pi͜u/	'lover or husband'	/pi/	'drink'

/i͜u/, /u/

/ji͜uwa/	'creature'	/juwa/	'gamble'

6. /e͜u/, /e/

/be͜ũt/	'device'	/bẽt/	'cane'
/ne͜uta/	'invitation'	/neta/	'leader'

/e͜u/, /u/

/de͜ur/	'husband's brother'	/dur/	'far'
/che͜u/	'cut'	/chu/	'touch'

7. /ə͜u/, /ə/

/mə͜ur/	'a sort of crown to be worn on marriage'	/mər/	'die'
/nə͜u/	'nine'	/nə/	'no'

/ə͜u/, /u/

/ghəu̯r/	'bunch'	/ghur/	'turn up'
/phẽkəu̯/	'would he throw?'	/phẽku/	'which is thrown'

8. /au̯/, /a/

/nau̯/	'boat'	/na/	'no'
/au̯/, /u/			
/chau̯/	'acting'	/chu/	'touch'

The contrast between diphthongs and vowel-sequences is not observed.

Phonological Structure and Distribution

On the basis of structure and distribution Magahī diphthongs are quite different from the sequence of vowels. Magahī diph. is a syllabic unit, constituted as a combination of two vocalic elements one of which is non-syllabic. On the other hand a sequence of vowels is a combination of two pure vowel phonemes. All diphs. end with either /i/ or /u/ where as no sequence of vowel is found which ends with these ones.

Almost all diphs. have as much frequency as the pure vowels. Most of the diphs. occur in all three, initial, medial and final positions. But the sequences of vowels are very much less frequent and their distribution is also restricted. (chap. 2.4). No sequence of vowels occurs initially except ia. Some of them take place only finally which are ie, ue and oe. The ea occurs only medially. Those sequences of vowels which occur medially and finally are oa, ua, iə, uə, iə, oe and uə.

Phonetic Features of Diphthongs

Diphthongs on Cardinal Vowel Diagram

The diphs. are shown on the following cardinal vowel diagram by cross marks from where they start to the direction of their second element. The arrows indicate the direction of tongue-motion during the pronunciation.

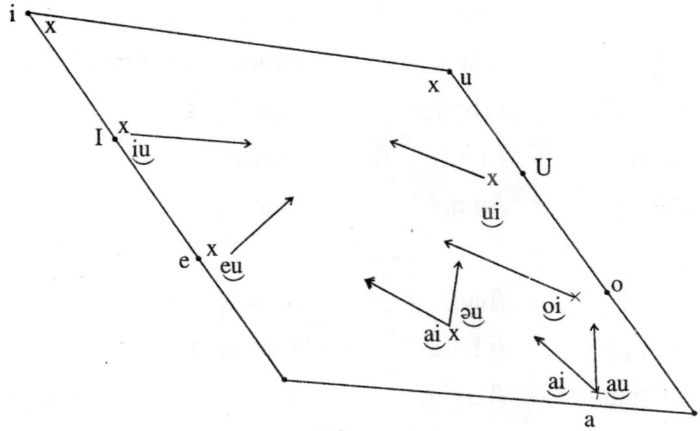

Diagram

Phonetic Description

Phonetically, for a Magahī diph. the vocal organs after producing a vocalic sound shift their position towards another sound which is called a glide that is, usually non-syllabic.

Every diph. goes to a close vowel, no one from close to open, *e.g.*, /ai/ and /au/ from open to close, /əi/ and /əu/ from half open to close, /iu/ and /ui/ from close to close and /eu/ oi/ from half close to close.

Distributional Remarks

The distribution of these diphs. is not similar. Some occur initially, medially as well as finally which can be found in the case of /əi oi/ and /əu/. /ai ui eu/ and /iu/ occur medially and finally. The diph. /iu/ is least frequent, however, it is observed in some words medially as well as finally. The distribution of /au/ is confined to final position only. Their distribution follows :

Distribution

1. /əi/

[əisən] /əisən/ 'like this'

[əis]	/əis/	'luxury'
[cəit]	/cəit/	'a month of spring'
[gh<əila.]	/ghəila/	'water pot'
[pəi]	/pəi/	'charge'
[bhəi]	/bhəi/	'fear'

2. /ai/

[bail]	/bail/	'outsider'
[ghail]	/ghail/	'wounded'
[lUgai/	/lUgai/	'wife'
[so.h̄ai]	/sohai/	'like'

3. /oi/

[oina·]	/oina/	'a name of a place
[loiya·]	/loiya/	'a round shape'
[khoicha·]	/khoicha/	'a bundle of presentation in sari'
[toi]	/toi/	'lace'
[soi/	/soi/	'sources of water'

4. /ui/

[r̄uiba·]	/ruiba/	'cotton'
[əpsuiya.]	/əpsuiya/	'unmarried girl'
[sui]	/suil/	'needle'
[ərui]	/ərui]	'a kind of vegetable'

5. /əu/

[əurət]	/əurət/	'woman'
[əugh<ər]	/əughər/	'obstinate'
[məuji·]	/məuji/	'jovial'

[cəu̯wa·]	/cəu̯wa/	'five fingers'
[g<əu̯]	/gəu̯/	'cow'
[ləu̯]	/ləu̯/	'flame'

6. /au̯/

[bhau̯]	/bhau̯/	'rate'
[nau̯]	/nau̯/	'bend down or boat'

7. /eu̯/

[deu̯ra·]	/deu̯ra/	'husband's brother'
[teu̯s]	/teu̯s/	'before last three year'
[neu̯]	/neu̯/	'foundation'
[kh<eu̯]	/kheu̯/	'rowing'

8. /iu̯/

[k<iu̯l]	/kiu̯l/	'the name of a town, a famous railway station'
[niu̯wa·]	/niu̯wa/	'foundation'
[gh<iu̯]	/ghiu̯/	'ghee'
[piu̯]	/piu̯/	'lover or husband'

Table 1 : Vowels with Allophones

	Front	*Central*	*Back*
High	i[i·] [i]		u[u.] [u]
Lower High	I[I]		U[U]
Mid	e[e.] [e]	ə[ə>] [ə.^] [ə]	o[o.] [o]
Low			a[a.] [a]

Diphthongs

Front off-glide	*Back off-glide*
ə͜i	ə͜u
a͜i	a͜u
o͜i	e͜u
u͜i	i͜u

Sequence of Vowels

Types of Sequence of Vowels

Magahī has four types of sequence of vowels[1] which are as under :

(i) v + v, (ii) v͜v+ v, (iii) v + v͜v and (iv) v͜v+ v͜v.

Phonetic Features of Sequence of Vowels

In the vowel-sequence of Magahī[2] a glide can be heard during the transition period when the tongue moves from one peak of prominence to another. There is actually, a sequence of only two syllabic vowels, *i.e.*, (i) not only in sequence of two vowels but in sequence of a diph. and a vowel or *vice-versa,* only two syllables are heard. (ii) Een in a combination of two diphs. there are only two syllables. Their distribution is given below :

Distribution

Sequences of two vowels

Sequences of two vowels have different varieties. They are twelve in number and end with /ə a o e/. Their distribution follows :

		Initial		*Medial*		*Final*	
1.	ia	/iar/	'friend'	/piãk/	'drunk-ard'	/pia/	'lover or husband'
		/iad/	'memory'	/niar/	'presen-tation'	/jia/	'heart'
2.	ea	x		/mear/	'a name of a village'	x	
		x		/teag/	'sacri-fice'	x	
3.	oa	x		/soakhən/	'wel-come'	/koa/	'palm-fruit'
		x		/poar/	'hay'	/dhoa/	'the name of a river'
4.	ua	x		/puar/	'hay'	/sua/	'big needle'
		x		/səsuar/	'father-in-law's house'	/jua/	'gamble'
5.	io	x		/biog/	'separa-tion'	/dio/	'may I give?'
6.	uo	x		/suog/	'chance'	/bhuo/	'to let it to be rotten'
		x		x		/juo/	'even gamble'
7.	ie	x		x		/pie/	'let him drink'

Contd...

	Initial	*Medial*		*Final*	
	x	x		/hĩe/	'here'
8. ue	x	x		/cue/	'let it leak'
	x	x		/bhuẽ/	'earth'
9. oe	x	x		/dhoe/	'let it to be washed'
	x	x		/roe/	'let him weep'
10. iə	x	/piət/	'drink'	/siə/	'stitch/,
		/siət/	'stitch'	/jiə/	'live long'
11. oə	x	/dhoəl/	'washed'	/dhoə/	'wash'
		/roəl/	'wept'	/boə/	'sow'
12. uə	x	/ṭuər/	'orphen'	/chuə/	'touch'
		/duəri/	'door'	/cuə/	'leak'

Sequences of a Diphthong and a Vowel

Mainly they are of two types : (a) diph. + vowel and (b) vowel + diph. Their distribution as in :

(a)	*Initial*		*Medial*		*Final*	
1. ə͜ie	x		x		/nə͜ie/	'boat'
2. ə͜io	/ə͜io/	'shall I come?'	x		/ḳə͜io/	'so many'
3. ə͜iạ	x		kə͜iạl/	'mossed/	/mə͜ia/	'mother'
4. ə͜ue	x		x		/cə͜ue/	'the four fingers'

Contd...

Contd...

5. əuo	x	x		/ḍhəuo/	'even coin'
6. əua	x	/bəual/	'misled'	/kəua/	'crow'
7. iua	x	x		/ghiua/	'ghee'
8. eue	x	x		/seue/	'apple'
9. euo	x	x		/seuo/	'even apple'
10.eua	x	x		/seua/	'apple'
11.oie	x	x		/khoie/	'outer part of fruit'
12.oio	x	x		/soio/	'do I sleep?'
13.oia	x	/loial/	'being rounded'	/soia/	'sources of water'
14.uie	x	x		/kuĩe/	'well'
15.uio	x	x		/kuĩo/	'even well'
16.uia	x	x		/buia/	'a subject of fear'

Sequences of vowel and a diphthong

They never occur initially.

(b)	*Medial*	*Final*	
17. iai	x	/biai/	'let her give birth'
18. iəu	x	/liəu/	'would I take?'

Contd...

Contd...

19. ia͜u	x		/hia͜u/	'courage'
20. iə͜i	/khịə͜ila/	'decayed'	/jiə͜i/	'live'
21. ea͜i	x		/rea͜i/	'concession'
22. ea͜u	x		/lea͜u/	'bring'
23. oə͜i	x		/roə͜i/	'would he weep?'
24. oa͜i	x		/roa͜i/	'weeping'
25. oə͜u	x		/hoə͜u/	'let it happen'
26. oa͜u	x		/dhoa͜u/	'wash'
27. uə͜i	/dhũə͜il/	'smoked'	/cuə͜i/	'let it leak'
28. ua͜i	x		/dhũa͜i/	'let it to be smoked'
29. uə͜u	x		/cuə͜u/	'let it leak'
30. ua͜u	x		/bhua͜u/	'let it to be rotten'

Sequences of two Diphthongs

Sequences of two diphthongs are as under : These do not occur medially.

		Initial		*Final*	
1	ə͜iə͜i	/ə͜iə͜i/	'would I come?'	/khə͜iə͜i/	'would I eat?'
2.	ə͜iə͜u	/ə͜iə͜u/	'would I come?'	/khə͜iə͜u/	'would I eat?'
3.	ə͜ua͜u	x		/bə͜ua͜u/	'let him to be dreamed'

Contd...

Contd...

4.	ə͜ua͜i	x	/bə͜ua͜i/	-do-
5.	o͜iə͜u	x	/ro͜iə͜u/	'would I weep?'
6.	o͜iə͜i	x	/so͜iə͜i/	'would I sleep?'
7.	u͜iə͜u	x	/chu͜iə͜u/	'would I touch'
8.	u͜iə͜i	x	/chu͜iə͜i/	'would I touch'

Table 2 : Sequences of Vowels

1. v + v, 2. v͜v+ v, 3. v + v͜v, 4. v͜v + v͜v.

	i	e	ə	a	o	u	ə͜i	o͜i	a͜i	u͜i	ə͜u	e͜u	i͜u	a͜u
i		X	X	X	X		X		X		X			X
e				X					X					X
ə														
a														
o		X	X	X			X		X		X			X
u		X	X	X	X		X		X		X			X
ə͜i		X		X	X		X				X			
o͜i		X		X	X		X				X			
a͜i														
u͜i		X		X	X		X				X			
ə͜u		X		X	X				X					X
e͜u		X		X	X									
i͜u				X										
a͜u														

REFERENCES

1. (a) According to Dr. Sampatti Aryani Magahī has twelve vowels as अ, आ, इ, ई, उ, ऊ, ए, ऐ, ओ, औ, अँ and अं But her treatment and her results are based on devanāgarī orthography and not on spoken language—
Magahī Vyakaran Kosh—a part of the thesis of Patna University on Magahī language and literature for D. Litt. in 1964, p. 1.

   (b) In an inventory of the phonemes of Magahī Swarnalata Prasad also gives eight vowels as /i e ae əaɔ̄o u/ and length /:/. But so far as my data is conceerned, there is no phoneme like /ae, ɔ̄/ and /: /. Moreover, she does not mention anywhere diphthongs—
Juncture and Aitch in Magahī, Indian Linguistics, Turner Jubilee Volume II, 1959, p. 118.

2. *An Outline of English Phonetics,* Daniel Jones, 1962, p. 58.
3. The analysis of diph. and sequence of vowels is not evident in the thesis of Dr. Sampatti Aryani. Once / ə͜i/ and /ə͜u/ are assumed as diphs. however they take place as sequences of vowels.
Magahī Vyakarana Kosh : Dr. Sampatti Aryani, 1964, pp. 3-4.
4. A sequence of three vocoids of Magahī can not be analysed as triphthongs, because a triphthong is also a syllabic element which starts from one sound and moves through a second to a third sound within the same syllable. (*General Phonetics,* R-M.S. Heffner, 1952, p. 112). It possesses a peak of prominence. The analysis of the diphthongs, the triphthongs and the sequences of vowels is not very clear in the works of Hindi and Lahndi which have been made till now. These are :
   (a) *Evolution of Awadhi*, Dr. Babu Ram Saksena, 1937, pp. 83-84.
   (b) *Bhojpuri Bhasha Aur Sahitya*, Dr. U.N. Tiwari, 1954, p. 76.
   (c) *Hindi Bhasha Ka Itihas,* Dr. Dhirendra Verma, 1958, pp. 110-114.
   (d) *Braj Bhasha*, Dr. Dhirendra Verma, 1954, p. 41.
   (e) *Lahndi Phonetics,* Dr. Hardeo Bahri, 1963, p. 89.

4
CONSONANTS

Classification of Consonants

There are in all twenty-nine consonant phonemes in Magahī. These consonants can be differentiated on the basis of (i) points of articulation, and (ii) manner of articulation.

Phonetic Classification

Phonetically speaking there are seven different places of articulation which are : (i) bilabial, (ii) dental, (iii) alveolar, (iv) retroflex, (v) palatal, (vi) velar, and (vii) glottal. According to the manner of articulation the distinctions observed are eight in number : (i) stops, (ii) affricates, (iii) spirants, (iv) nasals, (v) lateral, (vi) trill, (vii) flap and (viii) frictionless continuants.

Phonemic Classification

Phonemically speaking there are not more than five distinctly contrastive features in any one row of sounds and hence, it is not necessary to postulate more than five distinct places of articulation in the language.

Points of Articulation

Thus, we have considered p, ph, b, bh, m and w as labials, t, th, d, dh, n, s, l and r as dentals, ṭ, ṭh, ḍ, ḍh and ṛ as retroflex, c, ch, j, jh and y as palatals, k, kh, g, gh and h as velars.

Manner of Articulation

As regards the mode of articulation the maximum contrast is six-fold, *i.e.*, (i) stops (inclusive of affricates), (ii) spirants,

(iii) nasals, (iv) lateral, (v) trill (inclusive of flap) and (vi) frictionless continuants.

Voiced vs. Unvoiced and Aspirated vs. Unaspirated

All oral stops, including affricates, show a distinction for voiced Vs. unvoiced on the one hand and aspirated Vs. non-aspirated on the other hand. Thus for example, a voiceless bi-labial stop has as its counterpart, a voiced bi-labial stop and as well as a voiced and unvoiced aspirated stop.

The voicing or unvoicing is irrelevant with regard to the remaining consonants including the nasals, *e.g.*,

spirants	:	s, h
lateral	:	l
nasals	:	m, n
trills	:	r, ṛ
frictionless conts.	:	w, y

General Remarks

Though, some so-called aspirated consonants as m-h, n-h, r-h, l-h and k-h, g-h, b-h have also been observed which are considered as clusters, not unit phonemes.

Almost all consonants occur initially, medially as well as finally except ṛ, w, y which are never seen initially.

These consonant phonemes are set up on the basis of contrast available, which are given below :

Consonant-Contrast

Position class

Labials

/p, ph, b, bh, m, w/

	Initial		
/pan/	'betel leaf'	/phan/	'jump'
/ban/	'arrow'	/bhan/	'feel'
/man/	'prestige' 'honour'		
	Medial		
/səpər/	'thinking'	/səphər/	'travelling'
/sobab/	'test'	/sobhab/	'nature'
/səmau/	'insert'	/səwar/	'decorate'
	Final		
/gəp/	'gossip'	/gəph/	'thick'
/dab/	'press'	/ḍabh/	'green coconut'
/dam/	'cost'		

Dentals

/t th d dh n s l r/

	Initial		
/tan/	'to tighten'	/than/	'a cloth-measurement'
/dan/	'donation'	/dhan/	'paddy'
/naj/	'pride'	/saj/	'decorate'
/laj/	'shyness'	/raj/	kingdom'
	Medial		
/nətIya/	'grandson/	/nəthIya/	'nose ring'
/nədIya/	'river'	/bədhIya/	'a religious thread'
/nənIya/	'grand mother'	/bəsurI/	'flute'

/bəlurI/	'remaining part'	/bəṛərI/	'celling'
	Final		
/mət/	'no'	/məth/	'to churn'
/məd/	'purpose'	/mədh/	'honey'
/mən/	'mind'	/bas/	'residence'
/bal/	'hair'	/bar/	'day of the week'

Retroflex

/ṭ ṭh ḍ ḍh ṛ/

	Initial		
/ṭəg/	'to move'	/ṭhəg/	'cheat'
/ḍəg/	'step'	/ḍhəg/	'loose'
	Medial		
/'həṭIya/	'village market'	/həṭhIya/	'persistency'
/həḍIya/	'bone'	/bəḍhIya/	'flood'
/bəṛIya/	'garden'		
	Final		
/kaṭ/	'cut'	/kaṭh/	'wood'
/bəḍ/	'very'	/bəḍh/	'grow'
/ləṛ/	'fight'		

Palatals

/c ch j jh y/

	Initial		
/can/	'moon'	/chan/	'roof'
/jan/	'life'	/jhan/	'sad'
	Medial		
/əcar/	'pickle'	/əchar/	'a hard shower or rain'

/majəl/	'washed'	/majhəl/	'younger'
/kajəl/	'collyrium'	/kayl/	'influenced'
	Final		
/bac/	'read'	/bach/	'sorting out'
/baj/	'time to time'	/bajh/	'falcon'

Velars

/k kh g gh h/

	Initial		
/kan/	'ear'	/khan/	'mine'
/gan/	'song'	/ghan/	'ill fame'
/han/	'disadvantage'		
	Medial		
/səktI/	'strength'	/səkhtI/	'hardness'
/əgor/	'wait'	/əghor/	'dirty'
/əhor/	'exchange'		
	Final		
/jõk/	'a sort of water-insect'	/jõkh/	'chance'
/jog/	'chance'	/magh/	'a month of winter'
/mah/	'month'		

Formation Class

Voiceless Stops

/p t ṭ c k/

	Initial		
/par/	'cross'	/tar/	'telegram', 'wire'

/ṭar/	'neglect'	/car/	'four'
/kar/	'black'		
	Medial		
/kəpar/	'head'	/kətar/	'line'
/kəṭar/	'dagger'	/əcar/	'pickle'
/əkar/	'size'		
	Final		
/bap/	'father'	/bat/	'matter'
/baṭ/	'way'	/bac/	'read'
/bak/	'sentence'		

Voiced stops

/b d ḍ j g/

	Initial		
/bəs/	'stop'	/dəs/	'ten'
/ḍəs/	'beat'	/jəs/	'fame'
/gəs/	'faint'		
	Medial		
/labəl/	'brought'	/ladəl/	'loaded'
/kajəl/	'collyrium'	/lagəl/	'fexed'
	Final		
/ab/	'faith'	/ad/	'memory'
/aj/	'to day'	/ag/	'fire'

Voiceless Aspirated Stops

/ph th ṭh ch kh/

	Initial		
/phan/	'jump'	/than/	'a sort of measurement'

/ṭhan/	'decision'	/chan/	'roof'
/khan/	'mine'		
	Medial		
/səphIya/	'cleaner'	/səthIya/	'friend'
/səṭhIya/	'sixty years old'	/gəchIya/	'plant'
/səkhIya/	'girl friend'		
	Final		
/kəph/	'bad saliva'	/kəth/	'catechu'
/kəṭh/	'wooden'	/kach/	'a water insect'
/kəkh/	'painful sound'		

Voiced Aspirated Stops

/bh dh ḍh jh gh/

	Initial		
/bhər/	'fill up'	/dhər/	'put down'
/ḍhər/	'to be kindful'	/jhər/	'give up'
/ghər/	'house'		
	Medial		
/abhIye/	'just now'	/ədhIye/	'smallest coin'
/majhəl/	'of paste'	/lãghəl/	'crossed'
	Final		
/labh/	'gain'	/badh/	'exclude'
/baḍh/	'growth'	/bajh/	'falcon'
/bagh/	'tiger'		

Nasals

/m n/

	Initial		
/mar/	'beating'	/nar/	'woman'

	Medial		
/bIman/	'aeroplane'	/bInan/	'knitting'
	Final		
/dham/	'sacred place'	/dhan/	'paddy'

Flap, Trill, Lateral

	/r ṛ l/		
	Initial		
/raj/	'kingdom'	/laj/	'shyness', 'shame'
	Medial		
/pərna/	'a religious performance'	/pəṛna/	'lay down'
/pəlna/	'cradle'		
	Final		
/har/	'defeat'	/haṛ/	'bone'
	/hal/	'news'	

Spirants

	/s h/		
	Initial		
/san/	'dignity'	/han/	'ill-fame'
	Medial		
/nəsa͜i/	'distroy'	/nəha͜i/	'bath'
	Final		
/as/	'hope'	/ah/	'cold breath', 'deep breath'

Frictionless Continuants

/w y/

	Medial		
/newar/	'a kind of big lace'	/neyar/	'presentation of sweet'
/rIwaj/	'custom'	/rIyaj/	'habit'
/sIwan/	'a name of a place'	/sIyan/	'stitching'
/dUwar/	'door'	/dIyar/	'sandy land within a river'
/pUwar/	'hay'	/pIyar/	'love'

Retroflex Voiced Stop Vs. Flap

/ḍ ṛ/

/hĨḍol/	'swing'	/hĨṛor/	'acute pain of stomach'
/ləḍUwa/	'motichur sweet'	/ləṛUwa/	'a sweet of rice flower'
/həḍIoya/	'bone'	/həṛIya/	'earthen pot'
/hUḍUk/	'the action of plunge'	/hUṛUk/	'swallow'

ALLOPHONICS

Stops

Unvoiced Unaspirated Stops

With regard to point of articulation there is a five-fold contrast in unvoiced stops including affricates. These are : (i) labial, (ii) dental, (iii) retroflex, (iv) palatal, and (v) velar. All the unvoiced stops have two allophones as (a) released[1] and (b) unreleased. The unreleased one occurs medially as the first element of cluster and the released one in all other places, except in case of /p/ the unreleased form occurs in final position as well.

Their detailed description is given below :

1. /p/ an unaspirated unvoiced bilabial stop. It has two allophones which are as in :–

[-p⁼]	[p⁼ə˃g˂əh̄a·]	/pəgəha/	'tether'
	[p⁼Uar]	/pUar/	'straw'
	[k˂əp⁼ur]	/kəpur/	'camphor'
	[cã·p⁼a·]	/cãpa/	'accident'
[ṗ']	[nap']	/nap/	'measure'
	[sUṛUp']	/sUṛUp/	'sip'
	[chəp'p⁼ər]	/chəppər/	'country made roof'
	[k˂əp'phən]	/kəpphən/	'shroud'
	[cəp'ṭ=a.]	/cəpṭa/	'disfigured'
	[səp'na.]	/səpna/	'dream'

2. /t/ an unaspirated unvoiced dental stop. It has the usual two allophones, *e.g.*,

[-t⁼]	[t⁼Iləuri·]	/tIləuri/	'pudding made of seeds'
	[t⁼o·t⁼əṛa·h̄a.]	/toəṛaha/	'strammer'
	[sət=e·l·a.]	/sətela/	'step' brother
	[t⁼at⁼əl]	/tatəl/	'hot'
	[bhut⁼]	/bhut/	'ghost'
	[lIya·k˂ət⁼]	/lIyakət/	'capacity'
[t']	[pUt't⁼Ul]	/pUttUl/	'puppet'
	[pət'thər]	/patthər/	'rock'

	[dUṭ'k⁼ar]	/dUtkar/	'chide'
	[k=o·ṭ'b⁼a·li·]	/kotbali/	'police station

3. /ṭ/ an unaspirated unvoiced retroflex stop. It has also the usual two allophones which are as below :

[ṭ⁼]	[ṭ⁼Uk<əli·]	/ṭUkəli/	'a small disk'
	[ṭ⁼əṭ⁼ə>k⁼a·]	/ṭəṭəka/	'fresh'
	[kh<əṭ⁼o·la·]	/khəṭola/	'small cot'
	[ləṭ⁼əpəṭ⁼]	/ləṭəpəṭ/	'unfair'
	[phũṭ⁼]	/phũṭ/	'discord'
	[clp⁼əṭ⁼]	/clpəṭ/	'catch up'
[ṭ']	[p⁼əṭ'ṭ⁼i·]	/pəṭṭi/	'bandage'
	[p⁼əṭ'ṭha.]	/pəṭṭha/	'strong'
	[gh<əṭ'na·]	/ghəṭna/	'incident'
	[nəṭ'k⁼a.]	/nəṭka/	'dwarf'

4. /c/ an unaspirated unvoiced palatal affricate. It has also the usual two allophones but the unreleased form [c'] occurs only in the cluster of homoorganic consonants, *e.g.*,

[c⁼]	[c⁼ək<əla·]	/cəkəla/	'pastry-board'
	[c⁼əura·]	/cəura/	'rice'
	[əc⁼ərəj⁼]	/əcərəj/	'wonder'
	[məc⁼Iya·]	/məcIya/	'country made easy chair'
	[noc⁼]	/noc/	'snatching'

	[phĩc=]	/phĩc/	'wash'
[c']	[bəc'‿c=a·]	/bəcca/	'child'
	[lUc'‿c=a·]	/lUcca/	'unfaithful', 'wiked'
	[k<əc'‿cha·]	/kəccha/	'underwear'
	[bəc'‿chər]	/bəcchər/	'year'

5. /k/an unaspirated unvoiced velar stop. In addition, whenever it is followed by front and central vowels, it has an advanced variety [k<] occuring initially and medially. Thus, along with the usual ones it has three allophones which are illustrated below :

[k=]	[k=al]	/kal/	'death'
	[k=o·ra·]	/kora/	'raw'
	[hə̃k=au̯]	/hə̃kau̯/	'call'
	[ṭhek=u̯a·]	/ṭhekua/	'a kind of sweet or pastry'
	[sĩk=]	/sĩk/	'stub'
	[p=alək=]	/palək/	'a kind of vegetable'
[k'.]	[cUk'‿·k=a·]	/cUkka/	'small earthen pot'
	[ə>k'‿kh<əṛ]	/əkkhəṛ/	'obstinate'
	[pho·k‿c=a·]	/phokca/	'waterbowl'
	[c=ə>k'‿t=a·]	/cəkta/	'spot'
[k<]	[k<in]	/kin/	'perchase'
	[k<e·la·]	/kela/	'banana'
	[c=Uk<Iya·]	/cUkIya/	'earthen toy'
	[c=əm‿k<əl]	/cəmkəl/	'brightened'

UNVOICED ASPIRATED STOPS

Aspiration

Phonetically the aspirated voiceless and voiced stops are made up of the stops followed by an aspiration in close succession. The aspirated stops indicate at least two possibilities of their interpretation. They may be analysed as (i) unit phonemes[2] or as (ii) clusters with /h/.[3] The most important evidence in this regard is to be found in a contrast between such aspirated stops and a stop followed by the aspiration h.

kh k – h.
gh g – h. *e.g.*,

[Uphəna·]	/Uphəna/	'to boil'
[Up-həna·]	/Upa-həna/	'to be disappeared'
[k<ə>kh<əra·]	/kəkhəra/	'a name of a village'
[k<ə>k-həra·]	/kək-həra/	'the alphabet'

In addition, they behave like single unit in their distribution and in the formation of clusters. The cluster-habit of the aspirated stops is illustrated below :

Final

[p=ənth]	/pənth/	'way'
[g<əndh]	/gəndh/	'smell'
[k<ənṭh]	/kənṭh/	'throat'
[lUnjh]	/lunjh/	'paralysed'

Here we are not in favour of another interpretation which has advantages of reducing phonemes to a considerable number. Only for the economy of inventory we cannot ignore the phonemic contrast and distributional factors mentioned above.[4]

While /ph th ṭh/ and /ch/ have only one allophone occuring initially, medially and finally, the back aspirated stops /kh/ has two varieties like other back stops.

Their description has been given below :

1. /ph/ an aspirated voiceless bi-labial stop. Its distribution follows :

[ph]	[phəne·la·]	/phənela/	'fig'
	[phə˃gUa·]	/phəgUa/	'a Hindu festival'
	[k.˂əp'‿phən]	/kəpphən/	'shroud'
	[ma·phi·]	/maphi/	'pardon'
	[bhãph]	/bhãph/	'steam'
	[hãph]	/hãph/	'throbbing'

2. /th/ an aspirated voiceless dental stop. *e.g.*,

[th]	[thak$^{=}$]	/thak/	'layer'
	[thə˃k$^{=}$]	/thək/	'to be tired'
	[ma·tha·]	/matha/	'head'
	[səthIya·]	/səthIya/	'friend'
	[g$^{=}$ath]	/gath/	'to be in thread'
	[k˂əth]	/kəth/	'catechu'

3. /ṭh/ an aspirated voiceless retroflex stop. *e.g.*,

[ṭh]	[ṭhi·k$^{=}$a·]	/ṭhika/	'contract'
	[ṭhəs]	/ṭhəs/	'weak'
	[p$^{=}$a·ṭha·]	/paṭha/	'he goat'
	[ã·ṭhi·]	/ãṭhi/	'fruit's stone'

	[g$^{=}$ãṭh]	/gãṭh/	'knot'
	[seṭh]	/seṭh/	'rich man', 'merchant'

4. /ch/ an aspirated voiceless palato-alveolar affricate. It is slightly forward than its unaspirated counter part owing to aspiration. It has only one allophone, occuring initially, finally as well as medially, *e.g.*,

[ch]	[chəl]	/chəl/	'cheat'
	[chik$^{=}$]	/chik/	'sneeze'
	[b$^{=}$a·cha·]	/bacha/	'calf'
	[məchli]	/məchəli/	'fish'
	[p$^{=}$ach]	/pach/	'scratch'
	[mõch]	/moch/	'moustache'

5. /kh/ an aspirated voiceless velar stop. It has two allophones *i.e.*, (i) the back quality and (ii) the advanced quality. The second one occurs initially and medially followed by front and central vowels and the first one elsewhere, *e.g.*,

[kh$^{<}$]	/kh$^{<}$ir]	/khir/	'a kind of sweet preparation with milk and rice'
	[bə$^{>}$kh$^{<}$e·ṛa·]	/bəkheṛa/	'complications'
	[kh$^{<}$ər]	/khər/	'fried'
	[kh$^{<}$əṭ$^{=}$məl]	/khəṭməl/	'bed-bugs'
[kh]	[khas]	/khas/	'special'
	[khur]	/khur/	'hoof'

[b$^{=}$ə$^{>}$kho·ri·]	/bəkhori/	'a lower caste'
[mə$^{>}$kha·na·]	/məkhana/	'a dry fruit'
[ãkh]	/ãkh/	'eye'
[jhə$^{>}$kh]	/jhəkh/	[to be irritated'

VOICED UNASPIRATED STOPS

In spite of the distinction between voiced and voiceless stops, a similarity to some extent, is found among them, not only on the basis of the point of articulation, but also in their allophonic variations.

Here also released and unreleased allophones exist as we have seen in their counter parts.

The detailed description follows :

1. /b/ an unaspirated voiced bi-labial stop. From the view point of voicing it is fully voiced because the voice starts much earlier to the closure. Finally, it is unvoiced excluding which there are the usual two allophones like the voiceless bi-labial stop. *e.g.*,

[b$^{=}$]	[b$^{=}$ər]	/bər/	'bridegroom'
	[b$^{=}$ə͜ina·]	/bə͜ina/	'presentation'
	[səb$^{=}$a·ri·]	/səbari/	'vehicle'
	[t$^{=}$əb$^{=}$əla·]	/təbəla/	'a musical instrument'
[b·]	[g$^{<}$əb'͜b$^{=}$ər]	/gəbbər/	'deaf'
	[ḍ$^{=}$əb'͜bha·]	/ḍəbbha/	'tender coconut'
	[səb'j$^{=}$a·]	/səbja/	'green colour'
	[t$^{=}$əb'na·]	/təbna/	'to be heated'

[ḅ·]	[roḅ']	/rob/	'impression'
	[j=əḅ']	/jəb/	'when'
	[g=a͜iḅ']	/ga͜ib/	'disappear'
	[siḅ']	/sib/	'worm river or insect'

2. /d/ an unaspirated voiced dental stop. It has the usual two allophones. *e.g.*,

[d=]	[d=əh̄əj=əl]	/dəhəjəl/	'teased'
	[d=i·ya·]	/diya/	'earthen lamp'
	[b=Id=a·na·]	/bIdana/	'pomegranate'
	[k<əd=o·ṛa·]	/kədoṛa/	'muddy water'
	[ched=]	/ched/	'hole'
	[gh<ə͜ud=]	/ghə͜ud/	'cluster of fruits'
[d]	[lə͜d'd=əl]	/ləddəl/	'loaded'
	[b=o·d͜'d=a·]	/bodda/	'fool'
	[b=əd'‿dhI]	/bəddhI/	'religious thread'
	[əd'‿na·]	/ədna/	'much ordinary'

3. /ḍ/ an unaspirated voiced retroflex stop. In an intervocalic position, a single /ḍ/ is rare, however, it is confined to a few words including borrowed words from English otherwise, it occurs in the cluster of homoorganic consonants, *e.g.*,

[həḍ=Iya·] 'bone'	/ləḍ=Uwa·/	'a kind of round sweet'
'hĪḍ=ol/ 'swing'	/re·ḍ=Io·/	'radio'

It also has the usual two allophones :–

[ḍ⁼]	[ḍ⁼al]	/ḍal/	'branch of tree'
	[ḍ⁼Irar]	/ḍirar/	'line'
	[g<ənḍ⁼a·]	/gənḍa/	'a number of four'
	[ləḍ'ḍ⁼u·]	ləḍḍu/	'a kind of round sweet'
	[kh<ənḍ⁼]	/khənḍ/	'house garden'
	[lənḍ⁼]	/lənḍ/	'a vulgar word for penis'
[ḍ']	[k<əb⁼əḍ'ḍ⁼i·]	/kəbəḍḍi/	'a kind of play'
	[həḍ· ḍ⁼a·]	/həḍḍa/	'lean'
	[g<əḍ' ḍha·]	/gəḍḍha/	'trench'
	[b⁼Uḍ' ḍha·]	/bUḍḍha/	'old man'

4. /j/ an unaspirated voiced palatal affricate. It has also the usual two allophones, *e.g.*,

[j⁼]	[j⁼ãgh]	/jãgh/	'thigh'
	[j⁼ələm]	/jələm/	'birth'
	[əj⁼ə>g⁼Ut]	/əjəgUt/	'wonder'
	[ləj⁼al]	/ləjal/	'shied'
	[saj⁼]	/saj/	'decorate'
	[səhej⁼]	/səhej/	'preserve'
[j']	[d⁼əro·j' j⁼a·]	/dərojja/	'the entrance room of house'
	[səj' j⁼əl]	/səjjəl/	'decorated'

	[b=Ij' ‿jhəl]	/ɓIjjhəl/	'rotten'
	[b=əj'‿jhəl]	/bəjjhəl/	'engaged'

5. /g/ an unaspirated voiced velar stop. There are the usual three allophones like unvoiced stop. *e.g.*,

[g=]	[g=a‿i]	/ga‿i/	'cow'
	[g=or]	/gor/	'fair complexion'
	[so·h̄a.g=a·]	/sohaga/	'a sort of mineral', 'borax'
	[sə>g=a‿i]	/səga‿i/	'marriage of a widow'
	[j=ə>g=]	/jəg/	'the world'
	[so·h̄ag=]	/sohag/	'fortune of woman'
[g']	[lə>g' ‿g=a·]	/ləgga/	'a long stick'
	[j=ə>g· ‿g<əl]	/jəggəl/	'risen'
	[b=ə>g· ‿ghi.]	/bəgghi/	'a cart of two horses'
	[b=o·g' ‿c=a·]	/bogca/	'worthless thing'
	[bhə>g' ‿tha·]	/bhəgtha/	'hurdle'
[g<]	[g<it]	/git/	'song'
	[g<əm‿cha·]	/gəmcha/	'country made tovel'
	[b=əg<e·ri·]	/bəgeri/	'a kind of small bird'
	[b=ə>g<ə‿irəh]	/bəgə‿irəh/	'etc.'

VOICED ASPIRATED STOPS

/bh dh/ and /jh/ have only one allophone occuring initially, medially and finally but /ḍh/ and /gh/ have two allophones of different varieties.

Their description in detail is given below :

1. /bh/ an aspirated voiced bi-labial stop. *e.g.*,

[bh]	[bhə$^{>}$g$^{<}$ət$^{=}$]	/bhəgət/	'devotee'
	[bhãj$^{=}$]	/bhãj/	'obstruction'
	[so·bha͜u]	/sobha͜u/	'nature'
	[g$^{=}$abhIn]	/gabhIn/	'pregnant animal'
	[əbhI·]	/əbhI/	'now'
	[j$^{=}$ibh]	/jibh/	'tongue'

2. /dh/ an aspirated voiced dental stop. *e.g.*,

[dh]	[dhərəna·]	/dhərəna/	'satyagrah'
	[dhIya·]	/dhIya/	'children'
	[a·dha·]	/adha/	'half'
	[b$^{=}$əd'͜dhi·]	/bəddhi/	'religious thread'
	[nadh]	/nadh/	'start'
	[g$^{<}$idh/	/gidh/	'vulture'

3. /ḍh/ an aspirated voiced retroflex stop. It has two allophone as (i) the aspirated voiced retroflex stop [ḍh] and (ii) the aspirated voiced retroflex flap [ṛh]. The first one occurs in every position but medially and finally, it takes place in homo-organic consonants cluster. The [ṛh] occurs medially and finally. Medially it is intervocalic. These are as under :

[ḍh]	[ḍhə$^{>}$k$^{<}$əna·]	/ḍhəkəna/	'cover of a pot'

	[ḍhal]	/ḍhal/	'shield'
	[g<əd’͜ḍha·]	/gəddha/	'ditch'
	[hən͜ḍha·]	/həndha/	'day light'
	[kh<ən͜ḍh]	/khənḍh/	'house garden'
	[sUn͜ḍh]	/sUnḍh/	'insect of rice'
[ṛh]	[p⁼iṛha·]	/piṛha/	'a small seat of wood'
	[mo·ṛha.]	/moṛha/	'table'
	[b⁼aṛh]	/baṛh/	'flood'
	[loṛh]	/loṛh/	'to gather'

4. /jh/ an aspirated voiced palatal affricate. It has only one allophone which occurs initially, and finally, *e.g.*,

[jh]	[jhəmar]	/jhəmar/	'insult'
	[jhor]	/jhor/	'curry'
	[o·jha·]	/ojha/	'superstitious man'
	[sã·jhe·]	/sãjhe/	'evening'
	[mĩjh]	/mijh/	'to extinguish' (as light)
	[sajh]	/sajh/	'honest'

5. /gh/ an aspirated voiced velar stop. There are the usual two allophones as a back quality and an advanced quality. The second one occuring initially and medially followed by front and central vowels and the first one elsewhere, *e.g.*,

[gh<]	[gh<ə̃>gh<əra·]	/ghə̃ghəra/	'a sort of petti-coat used by tribals'

	[ghIr]	/ghIr/	'to be sorrounded'
	[ə˃gh˂ən]	/əghən/	'a name of a month'
	[ma·gh˂I·]	/maghI/	'which belongs to a month of winter'
[gh]	[gha·ṭ˭a·]	/ghaṭa/	'loss'
	[ghor]	/ghor/	'much'
	[ə˃gha͜i̯]	/əghai/	'satisfied'
	[ə˃gho·rI]	/əghorI/	'dirty'
	[b˭agh]	/bagh/	'tiger'
	[megh]	/megh/	'rain'

SPIRANTS

There are two spirants in the dialect as /s/ and /h/. The glottal spirant /h/ is the only consonant in which oral cavity does not take active part. There is only one allophone of /s/ and two allophones of /h/ as voiceless [h] and voiced [ɦ].

Their descriptions follow :

/s/ a voiceless alveolar groove spirant. It occurs initially, medially as well as finally. e.g.

[s]	[səḅ']	/səb/	'all'
	[sẽt]	/sẽt/	'preserve'
	[hə̃sUli·]	/hə̃sUli/	'country made heavy necklace'
	[pəse·na·]	/pəsena/	'sweat'
	[pis]	/pis/	'press'
	[os]	/os/	'dew'

/h/ a voiceless glottal spirant. There are two allophones as voiced [h̄] and voiceless [h]. The first one occurs medially in between vowels V h V. The second one occurs elsewhere. It is more of a lenis in final position. *e.g.*,

[h̄]	[bəh̄e·li.]	/bəhəli/	'fowler'
	[bi·h̄ən]	/bihən/	'seed'
	[me·h̄ətər]	/mehətər/	'sweeper'
	[əhəsan]	/əhəsan/	'obligation'
[h]	[haI]	/hal/	'news'
	[hĩn]	/hin/	'inferior'
	[k<ə>k͜-həra·]	/kək-həra/	'alphabet'
	[g<e·l͜-ha·]	/gel-ha/	'stone'
	[cah]	/cah/	'desire'
	[k<əh/	/kəh/	'tell'

NASALS

There are only two nasal phonemes in Magahī which occur in initial, medial and final positions. /m/ has only one allophone and /n/ consists of five. According to the following different sorts of stops the alveolar nasal occurs generally in different varieties. As a matter of fact, each of the stops has its corresponding homoorganic nasal contoid as it is set up below :

Velar	:	4k	4kh	4g	4gh
Palatal	:	3c	3ch	3j	3jh
Retroflex	:	ṇṭ	ṇṭh	ṇḍ	ṇḍh
Dental	:	n̪t̪	n̪t̪h	n̪d̪	n̪d̪h
Bilabial	:	mp	mph	mb	mbh

In the articulation of these nasal components the soft palate is lowered and a homo-organic oral occlusion is observed.

/n/ voiced alveolar nasal. It has two types of allophone, *i.e.*, (i) which occurs in clusters and (ii) which occurs elsewhere. The first one contains four varieties, occuring as the first element of cluster, made up with the following corresponding homoorganic stops which are as in :

I	[4]	followed by velar stops.
II	[3]	followed by palatal stops.
III	[ṇ]	followed by retroflex stops.
IV	[n̪]	followed by dental stops.

Clusters of these nasals as first member occur medially and finally but in final position they have less frequency.

The second one alveolar [n] occurs elsewhere.

Their distribution follows :

I [4]

[sə<ŋk<ər]	/sənkər/	'Lord Śiva'
[ḍə>ŋk]	/ḍənk/	'beat'
[pə>ŋkh<i·]	/pənkhi/	'feather'
[pə>ŋkh]	/pəmkh/	'feather'
[k<ə>ŋgal]	/kəngal/	'beggar'
[rə>ŋg]	/rəng/	'colour'
[k<ə>ŋgh<i·]	/kənghi/	'comb'
[sə>ŋgh]	/səngh/	'association'

II. [3]

[bə3cər]	/bəncər/	'fool'
[pə·3c]	/pənc/	'a union of five men'
[pə·3chi·]	/pənchi/	'Bird'

	Phonetic	Phonemic	Gloss
	[pəʒja·]	/pənja/	'five fingers'
	[g<əʒj]	/gənj/	'a place', 'a market'
	[səʒjha.]	/sənjha/	'of evening'
	[lUʒjh]	/lUnjh/	'paralised'
III.	[ṇ]		
	[əṇṭi]	/əṇṭi/	'a bundle of thread'
	[əṇṭ-səṇṭ]	/əṇṭsəṇṭ/	'worthless'
	[k<əṇṭhi·]	/kəṇṭhi/	'a religious thread worn around the neck'
	[ləṇṭh]	/ləṇṭh/	'fool'
	[kh<əṇḍa·]	/khəṇḍa/	'house garden'
	[jhUṇḍ·]	/jhUṇḍ/	'group'
	[ləṇḍha·]	/ləṇḍha/	'without tail'
	[sUṇḍh]	/sUṇḍh/	'a person who does not drink water'
IV.	[n̪]		
	[pən̪tal]	/pəntal/	'watery rice'
	[ən̪t]	/ənt/	'end'
	[sən̪thal]	/sənthal/	'a tribe'
	[pən̪th]	/pənth/	'way'
	[phən̪da·]	/phənda/	'net'
	[bən̪d]	/bənd/	'closed'
	[kh<ən̪dha·]	/khəndha/	'house garden'
	[g<ən̪dh]	/gəndh/	'smell'

V. [n]

[nəs]	/nəs/	'vein'
[nind]	/nind/	'sleep'
[pəna·la·]	/pənala/	'drainage'
[sənal]	/sənal/	'over-ripe'
[phən]	/phən/	'hood' (of a serpent)
[bIyãn]	/bIyãn/	'birth'

/m/ voiced bi-labial nasal occurs initially, medially as well as finally, *e.g.*,

[m]	[mər]	/mər/	'die'
	[mũh]	/muh/	'mouth'
	[əma·ri·]	/əmari/	'dry pieces of cow dung'
	[k<əmIỹa·]	/kəmiya/	'labourer'
	[cəmpa·]	/cəmpa/	'a flower'
	[simbh]	/simbh/	'a sort of vegetable'
	[nam]	/nam/	'name'
	[ṭIm-ṭIm]	/ṭIm-ṭIm/	'twinkle'

LATERAL AND TRILLS

Lateral

Magahī lateral is a voiced alveolar consonant. It is the most sonorous sound. Though /1/ contrasts with trill /r/, in some positions it is in free variation also. *e.g.*,

/həl/	/hər/	'plough'
/jəl/	/jər/	'burn'
/ḍal/	/ḍar/	'branch of tree'

/kela/	/kera/	'banana'

It has only one allophone occuring initially, medially as well as finally, *e.g.*,

[l]	[li·la·]	/lila/	'the play of God'
	[log]	/log/	'people'
	[ləl͜k<i·]	/ləlki/	'red coloured'
	[əlUwa·]	/əlUwa/	'potato'
	[k<əlol]	/kəlol/	'a play with water'
	[phul]	/phul/	'flower'

Trills

There are two sorts of trill phonemes *i.e.* /r/ and /ṛ/. Those have greater number of trills are greater in resonance. On the basis of number of trills these sounds are divided in their allophonic qualities. Phonetically /r/ is a result of two or three rapid succession of tapes of tongue against alveolar ridge. In flap consonant /ṛ/ the back tip of tongue goes up and tapes only once on the prepalatal region, that is slightly higher than /ṭ/. It never occurs initially.

Both are observed in free variation also. *e.g.*,

/məror/	/məṛor/	'pain of stomach'
/Irot/	/Iṛot/	'side'
/hUlar/	/hUlaṛ/	'fox'

Their allophonic description follows :

/r/ a voiced trill alveolar consonant. It has two allophones as (i) the greater number of trill and (ii) the smaller number of trill. The first one occurs initially followed by vowel and intervocally in gemination as the first contoid. The second one elsewhere.

[r̄]	[r̄as]	/ras/	'a kind of religious play'
	[r̄əs]	/rəs/	'juice'
	[r̄og]	/rog/	'disease'
	[r̄r̄k]	/rẽk/	'rough voice'
	[hər̄r̄e·]	/hərre/	'a sort of myrobalan'
	[kh<ər̄r̄a·]	/khərra/	'fair'
	[jhUr̄r̄i·]	/jhUrri/	'wrinkle'
	[ṭhər̄r̄a·]	/ṭhərra/	'a kind of skin disease'
[r]	[k<ərUwa·]	/kərUwa/	'bitter'
	[pẽrəl]	/pẽrəl/	'disatisfied'
	[k<ər]	/kər/	-do-
	[ə̃car]	/əc̃ar/	'pickles'
	[bhir]	/bhir/	'near'

/ṛ/ a voiced retroflex flap. It has only one allophone occuring medially and finally.

[ṛ]	[ə̃ṛəl]	/ə̃ṛəl/	'stuck'
	[məṛai̯]	/məṛai̯/	'hut'
	[məṛo.ṛa·]	/məṛora/	'stomach pain'
	[Uṛ]	/Uṛ/	'fly'
	[maṛ]	/maṛ/	'rice water'
	[dəu̯ṛ]	/dəu̯ṛ/	'run'

FRICTIONLESS CONTINUANTS

There are two frictionless continuants as /w y/ which occur only in intervocalic position. Each of them is voiced and has no allophone.

/w/ is voiced bilabial frictionless continuant. In its articulation the lips touch each other at their corners and a sort of constricted opening remains through which air passes.

/y/ is voiced palatal frictionless continuant, jaw being in the position similar to the articulation of /i/.

Their distribution follows :

/w/	[kŨwar]	/kŨwar/	'unmarried'
	[jUwãn/	/jUwan/	'young'
	[dewər]	/dewər/	'husband's younger brother'
	[k<əu̯wa·]	/kəu̯wa/	'crow'
	[dUwa·ri·]	/dUwari/	'door'
	[sə̃wər]	/sə̃wər/	'decorate'
/y/	[Iyar]	/Iyar/	'friend
	[piyər]	/piyər/	'yellow'
	[niyət]	/niyət/	'intention'
	[g<əya·]	/gəya/	'a famous holy place for Hindus'
	[bhu̯iyã·]	/bhu̯iyã/	'earth'
	[sa·ya·]	/saya/	'petticoat'

Table 3 ; Consonants with Allophones

		Labial	Dental	Retroflex	Palatal	Velar
	un-vd.	p	t	ṭ	c	k
	unasp.	[p⁼] [p’]	[t⁼][t’]	[ṭ⁼] [ṭ’]	[c⁼] [c’]	[k⁼] [k’] [k˂]
S	unvd.	ph	th	ṭh	ch	kh
T	asp.	[ph]	[th]	[ṭh]	[ch]	[kh] [kh˂]
O	vd.	b	d	ḍ	j	g
P	unasp.	[b⁼] [b’] [ḅ’]	[d⁼] [d’]	[ḍ⁼] [ḍ’]	[j⁼] [j’]	[g⁼] [g’] [g˂]
	vd.	bh	dh	ḍh	jh	gh
	asp.	[bh]	[dh]	[ḍh] [ṛh]	[jh]	[gh] [gh˂]
Spi-	unvd.					
ra-			s			h
nt			[s]			[h] [h]
Na-	vd.	m	n			
sal		[m]	[4] [3] [ṇ] [ṇ] [n]			
Late-		l				
ral	vd.	[l]				
Trill	vd.	ʳ[r̃][r]	ʳ[ṛ]			
Tric.	vd.					
conts						h

CLUSTERS

Types of clusters : Medial and Final

A consonant cluster of Magahī is a sequence of two or three consonants which occurs only medially and finally. No example is found of initial cluster.

Medial Cluster

Two Consonant Cluster

At first these clusters might be divided into two classes : (i) clusters of different consonants and (ii) clusters of the same consonants.

The first one consists of different types which are : (a) stop + stop, (b) stop + other consonants, (c) spirant + other consonants, (d) Nasal + other consonants, (e) lateral + other consonants, (f) trill + other consonants.

The clusters of the second variety contain geminated consonants, *i.e.*, t + t, l + I, r + r, etc.

On the other hand these clusters may be descriminated on the basis of syllabic division. The final clusters are quite independent to the medial ones. The compound consonants of final clusters cannot be divided into two syllables. *e.g.*, In /cənṭh/ 'wicked' cluster nṭh forms the coda of a syllable.

But medial clusters are intercepted as a syllable-boundary, first element as coda of the preceding syllable and second as on set of the following syllable :

(i) Syllable-boundary can fall between two different sorts of consonants. *e.g.*,

[ləm‿ba·]	/ləmba/	'long'
[k˂əp'‿ṭi·]	/kəpṭi/	'earthen cup'
[pət'‿la·]	/pətla/	'lean and thin'

(ii) Syllable-division can take place within the intervocalic gemination also. *e.g.*,

[həḍ'‿ḍi·]	/həḍḍi/	'bone'

[nəp'pa·]	/nəppa/	'measurement'
[cUl-lU]	/cUllU/	'handful'
[jUt'ta·]	/jUtta/	'shoe'

Three Consonant Clusters

In some cases, medially, the clusters of three consonants may be found but these are not very frequent. Evidently, it can be heard in rapid speech. Mostly these clusters are followed by long vowels and are preceded by short vowels.

The syllabic-division within the three consonant clusters takes place after the first element, *e.g.*,

[jən-tri·]	/jəntri/	'an object of superstition'
[bən-dri·]	/bəndri/	'she monkey'
[əl-blal·]	/əlblal/	'off minded'
[jən-mla·]	/jənmla/	'please take birth'

General Remarks

Medially almost all stops can occur as first element of cluster. All the clusters which begin with stop have their homoorganic aspirated forms also as the second member.

No cluster begins either with aspirated stops or with /h/. Frictionless continuents never form a cluster with any consonant.

Those beginning with bi-labials, affricates and velars have wider distribution.

Cluster with /n/ has wide range of consonant occuring as second element.

Aspirated consonants never occur in gemination. Geminated clusters are formed of all consonants except aspirated stops and /h ṛ/.

Final Clusters

Final clusters are few in number in comparison with medial clusters.

All these clusters occur in medial position as well.

Among geminated clusters only [c͜c] occurs in final position.

There are three types of final clusters :

(a) stop + stop

(b) spirant + stop

(c) nasal + stop or spirant

Nasal clusters occur more frequently than non-nasal clusters.

Examples

These clusters are illustrated below which have been shown also in table 4 and 5.

Medial Clusters

(a) stop + stop :

p + ph	:	/kəpphən/	'shroud'
p + t	:	/həpta/	'week'
p + ṭ	:	/kəpṭi/	'earthen cup'
p + c	:	/kə̃pcəl/	'cut'
p + ch	:	/Upchəl/	'empty'
p + j	:	/Upjəl/	'grown'
p + k	:	/jhəpkəl/	'dozen'
b + bh	:	/ḍəbbha/	'green coconut'
b + dh	:	/ləbdhəl/	'clung'
b + j	:	/kəbja/	'occupy'

b + jh	:	/ləbjhəl/	'clung'
t + ch	:	/lətchUt/	'infection'
t + th	:	/pətthər/	'stone'
t + k	:	/tItki/	'piece of fire'
d + dh	:	/bəddhi/	'a religious thread'
d + k	:	/lUdkəl/	'going fast'
ṭ + ṭh	:	/məṭṭha/	'butter milk'
ṭ + k	:	/məṭkəl/	'walking at ease'
ḍ + ḍh	:	/gəḍḍha/	'ditch'
c + ch	:	/gUccha/	'bunch'
c + k	:	/ləcka/	'a traditional conveyance'
j + jh	:	/bəjjhəl/	'engaged'
j + k	:	/bəjkəl/	'rotten'
k + b	:	/ləkba/	'paralysis'
k + t	:	/cəkta/	'a spot of body'
k + ṭ	:	/nəkṭi/	'nose dirt'
k + kh	:	/ləkkhəl/	'seen'
g + b	:	/ləgba/	'stick'
g + c	:	/bogca/	'a bundle of things'
g + j	:	/məgji/	'lace'
g + gh	:	/bəgghi/	'a two horse carriage'

(b) Stop + other consonants :

p + m	:	/upma/	'simile'
p + n	:	/səpna/	'dream'
p + r	:	/cəpra/	'kind of Lac'
p + s	:	/kə̃psəl/	'wept'
p + l	:	/dhəpla/	'trick'
p + ṛ	:	/kəpṛa/	'cloth'
p + h	:	/səp-ha/	'a place where snakes live'
b + n	:	/ləbni/	'an earthen pot'
b + r	:	/ḍhIbra/	'a name of village'
b + ṛ	:	/ləbṛa/	'tale bearer'
t + n	:	/gotni/	'sister-in-law'
t + r	:	/pətra/	'the religious book of astronomy'
t + l	:	/pətla/	'lean & thin'
d + n	:	/godna/	'black spot'
d + l	:	/bədla/	'revenge'
ṭ + n	:	/nəṭni/	'tale bearer woman'
j + n	:	/pəcbəjna/	'a traditional musical set of five'
k + n	:	/thUkni/	'woman who spits much'

k + s :	/bəksa/	'box'
k + c: :	/sIkca/	'a shackle'
k + h :	/pok-ha/	'a kind of small fruit'
g + h :	/Ug+hən/	'rop'

(c) spirant + other consonants :

s + b :	/desba/	'country'
s + p :	/dilcəspi/	'interest'
s + t :	/sə̃sta/	'cheap'
s + th :	/əsthan/	'place'
s + ṭ :	/bIsṭi/	'underwear'
s + j :	/məsjid/	'mosque'
s + k :	/cəska/	'habit'
s + g :	/pə̃sga/	'a sort of weight'
s + kh :	/noskha/	'prescription'
s + m :	/cəsma/	'spectacles'
s + r :	/pəsrəl/	'spread'
s + l :	/təsla/	'a kitchen pot'

(d) nasal + other consonants :

m + p :	/cəmpa/	'a kind of flower'
m + b :	/əmba/	'mango'
m + ph :	/ləmpha/	'lantern'
m + bh :	/khəmbha/	'pol'
m + t :	/bəmtal/	'out of control'

m + d	:	/əmdi/	'person'
m + ṭ	:	/sImṭəl/	'constracted'
m + ṭh	:	/səmṭha/	'a thick stick'
m + c	:	/ghəmci/	'prickly heat'
m + ch	:	/gəmchi/	'country made toble'
m + k	:	/jhUmka/	'a sort of earring'
m + n	:	/ləmna/	'an earthen pot'
m + s	:	/Umsəl/	'topped'
m + r	:	/ləmri/	'a tenor'
m+l	:	/gəmla/	'an earthen pot'
m + h	:	/ləmhər/	'tall'
n + t	:	/pəntal/	'watery rice'
n + th	:	/sənthal/	'a tribe of Bihar'
n + d	:	/unda/	'good'
n + dh	:	/kəndha/	'shoulder'
n + ṭ	:	/kənṭop/	'a cap covering the ears'
n + ṭh	:	/kənṭhi/	'a religious garland'
n + ḍ	:	/pənḍa/	'who conducts the religious performance', 'priest'
n + ḍh	:	/hənḍha/	'day light'
n + c	:	/pəncər/	'leaked'
n + ch	:	/pənchi/	'bird'
n + j	:	/mənjər/	'the blooms'

n + jh : /mənjha/ 'a kind of paste for thread'

n + k : /cənkəl/ 'broken'

n + kh : /unkha/ 'his'

n + g : /munga/ 'sort of vegetable'

n + m : /kənma/ 'ear'

n + r : /bənra/ 'monkey'

n + s : /phUnsi/ 'a pimple'

n + h : /kənhai/ 'a popular name'

n + k : /sənkha/ 'a conch shell'

n + kh : /pənkhi/ 'feather'

n + g : /gənga/ 'the biggest river of India'

n + gh : /kənghi/ 'comb'

(e) lateral + other consonants :

l + b : /məlba/ 'a cup for oil'

l + ph : /kulphi/ 'a sort of cup'

l + t : /səltal/ 'calm'

l + th : /pəlthi/ 'to sit cross legged'

l + d : /həldi/ 'a sort of red powder'

l + ṭ	:	/ulṭəl/	'converted'
l + c	:	/ləlcəl/	'greedy'
l + ch	:	/kəlchul/	'a kitchen article'
l + j	:	/Iljam/	'charge'
l + jh	:	/Uljhəl/	'complex'
l + k	:	/məlka/	'lightning'
l + kh	:	/bəlkhai̯/	'fluctuate'
l + g	:	/əlgal/	'protuberance'
l + m	:	/jəlməl/	'born'
l + n	:	/belna/	'a rolling tool of kitchen'
l + r	:	/bəlrI/	'insubstantial part'
l + s	:	/kəlsi/	'a small water pot'
l + h	:	/kUlhi/	'a sort of cap'

(f) trill + other consonants :

r + p	:	/khUrpi/	'a sickle for grass cutting'
r + ph	:	/bərphi/	'a sort of sweet'
r + b	:	/cərbi/	'fat'
r + t	:	/pərta/	'adjustment'
r + th	:	/sərtha/	'a name of a village'

r + d	:	/jərda/	'a variety of tobacoo'
r + dh	:	/sərdha/	'affection'
r + c	:	/kIrcI/	'a bundle of thread'
r + ch	:	/bərcha/	'a kind of arm'
r + j	:	/mərji/	'choice'
r + jh	:	/mUrjhal/	'fadup'
r + k	:	/bərkəl/	'decayed'
r + kh	:	/cərkha/	'carkha'
r + g	:	/mUrgi/	'hen'
r + gh	:	/kərgha/	'a sort of wheel'
r + m	:	/bərma/	'a sort of needle'
r + n	:	/bərna/	'but'
r + s	:	/porsa/	'a measurement of depth'
r + h	:	/bərha/	'a number of twelve'
ṛ + k	:	/sUṛkəl/	'sipped'
ṛ + s	:	/sə̃ṛsi/	'an instrument of goldsmith'

Clusters of the same consonants

p + p	:	/chəppər/	'thatch'
b + b	:	/nəbbəl/	'down'
t + t	:	/pətta/	'leaf'

d + d	:	/bodda/	'fool'
ṭ + ṭ	:	/khəṭṭa/	'sour'
ḍ + ḍ	:	/həḍḍa/	'lean and thin'
c + c	:	/gəcca/	'ditch'
j + j	:	/səjjəl/	'furnished'
k + k	:	/pəkka/	'floor'
g + g	:	/ləgga/	'stick'
m + m	:	/nəmma/	'name'
n + n	:	/nənna/	'grand father'
s + s	:	/ləssa/	'lust'
r + r	:	/hUrra/	'blow'
l + l	:	/gUlla/	'a bit of sugercane'

Clusters of three consonants

p + c + n	:	/kəpcna/	'hair cutting'
l + b + l	:	/əlblal/	'off minded'
n + p + u	:	/pənpnal/	'sharply'
n + t + r	:	/jəntri/	'an object of superstition'
n + d + r	:	/bəndri/	'she monkey'
n + m + l	:	/jənmla/	'please take birth'

Final Clusters

n + t	:	/sənt/	'saint'

n + th	:	/pənth/	'way'
n + d	:	/mənd/	'slow'
n + dh	:	/gəndh/	'smell'
n + ṭ	:	/sənṭ/	'neglect'
n + ṭh	:	/kənṭh/	'neck'
n + ḍ	:	/lənḍ/	'vulgar word for penis'
n + ḍh	:	/sənḍh/	'one who eats much'
n + c	:	/pənc/	'the committee of five'
n + j	:	/rənj/	'anger'
n + jh	:	/lUnjh/	'paralysed'
n + k	:	/rənk/	'poor'
n + kh	:	/sənkh/	'a couch shell'
n + g	:	/səng/	'with'
n + gh	:	/səngh/	'association'
n + s	:	/həns/	'swan'
n + h	:	/kanh/	'Lord Krishna'

(a) stop + stop :

p + t	:	/jəpt/	'confiscated'
kh + t	;	/səkht/	'hard'
k + th	:	/kətth/	'catechu'
c + c	:	/bucc/	'earless'

(b) Spirant + Stop :

s + t	:	/məɜt/	'happy', 'carefree'

Table 4 : Medial Clusters

		1	2	3	4	5	6	7	8	9	10	11	12	13	14	15	16	17	18	19	20	21	22	23	24	25	26	27	28	29
		p	t	ṭ	k	ph	th	ṭh	kh	b	d	ḍ	g	bh	dh	ḍh	gh	c	ch	j	jh	s	h	m	n	l	r	ṛ	w	y
1	p	x	x	x	x	x							x					x	x	x		x	x	x	x	x	x	x		
2	t		x		x		x												x						x	x	x			
3	ṭ			x	x			x																	x					
4	k		x	x	x				x	x								x				x	x		x					
5	ph																													
6	th																													
7	ṭh																													
8	kh																													
9	b								x				x		x					x	x				x		x	x		
10	d				x					x			x	x						x			x		x	x				
11	ḍ									x		x				x	x	x		x		x								
12	g									x			x				x	x		x			x							
13	bh																													
14	dh																													
15	ḍh																													
16	gh																													
17	c				x													x	x											
18	ch																													
19	j				x														x	x			x								
20	jh																													
21	s	x	x	x	x		x		x	x			x						x		x		x		x	x				
22	h																													
23	m	x	x	x	x	x	x	x		x	x			x			x	x			x	x	x	x	x	x				
24	n		x	x	x		x	x	x		x	x	x		x		x	x	x	x	x	x	x	x		x				
25	l		x	x	x	x	x		x	x	x		x				x	x	x	x	x	x	x	x	x	x				
26	r	x	x		x	x	x		x	x	x	x	x	x		x	x	x	x	x	x	x	x	x		x				
27	ṛ				x																									
28	w																													
29	y																													

Table 5 : Final Clusters

		1	2	3	4	5	6	7	8	9	10	11	12	13	14	15	16	17	18	19	20	21	22	23	24	25	26	27	28	29
		p	t	ṭ	k	ph	th	ṭh	kh	b	d	ḍ	g	bh	dh	ḍh	gh	c	ch	j	jh	s	h	m	n	l	r	ṛ	w	y
1	p		x																											
2	t																													
3	ṭ																													
4	k						x																							
5	ph																													
6	th																													
7	ṭh																													
8	kh		x																											
9	b																													
10	d																													
11	ḍ																													
12	g																													
13	bh																													
14	dh																													
15	ḍh																													
16	gh																													
17	c																	x												
18	ch																													
19	j																													
20	jh																													
21	s		x																											
22	h																													
23	m																													
24	n		x	x	x		x	x	x		x	x	x		x	x	x	x		x	x	x	x							
25	l																													
26	r																													
27	ṛ																													
28	w																													
29	y																													

REFERENCES

1. In this sub-section, the released variety of unasp. stops is marked as [p⁼] to distinguish it from unreleased variety, *e.g.*, [p']. In rest of the material this distinction is not indicated in the phonetic transcription.
2. *Bharat ki Bhashayon me Mahapran Byanjan* : William Brite, Hindi Anushilan, Dhirendra Verma Visheshank, 1960, pp. 16-20.
3. *Juncture and Aitch in Magahī* : Swarnalata Prasad, Indian Linguistics, Turner Jubilee Volume II, 1959, p. 118.
4. *The Phonemes of Bengali,* Charles A. Ferguson and Munir Chowdhury, Language, Volume 36, 1960, p. 47.

5
SYLLABIC STRUCTURE

Introductory

A syllable is defined as 'a peak of prominance,[1] or as 'a motor unit' that is, a puff of air forced upward through the vocal channel by a compression of the inter-costal muscles.[2]

Syllable Patterns

The syllable of Magahī is a vocalic unit or a combination of the vocalic unit preceeded or followed by consonants. It is assumed as short or long and pure or diph. It can be nasalized also.

The syllabic pattern of the language provides different varieties which are as under :

1. v	:	/i/	'this'	/u/	'that'
2. vc	:	/əṛ/	'to insist'	/ãkh/	'eye'
3. vcv	:	/əbhI/	'just now'	/Uṭhə/	'please get up'
4. vvc	:	/Iad/	'memory'	/Iar/	'friend'
5. vcc	:	/əng/	'organ'	/Inc/	'inch'
6. cv	:	/nə/	'no'	/dho/	'wash'
7. cvc	:	/ghər/	'house'	/bUl/	'walk'
8. cvcc	:	/lUnjh/	'paralysed'	/kənṭh/	'throat'
9. vccv	:	/əkṛa/	'rough rice'	/UllU/	'owl'
10. vcccv	:	/Ungli/	'finger'	/əntra/	'an element of music'

11.	cvv :	/rua/	'cotton'	/roe/	'let him weep'
12.	cvvc :	/puar/	'hay'	/suər/	'swine'

Syllable-Division

The division of Magahī syllable, as a matter of fact, is the division of chest pulses one from another.[3] An attempt has been made here to fix up some rules regarding the syllable-division which follow :

In non-monosyllabic words of (c) vcv (c) pattern the syllable division comes before medial consonants. For instance in /raja/ 'king', the cut takes place before /j/ because the length of the nucleus of the first syllable goes to that extent till the medial consonant begins. Some more examples :

/a-ri/ 'saw' /ə-gIn/ 'fire'

/ka-jəl/ 'collyrium'

In the sequence of two consonants, in pattern /vccv/, the syllable division comes usually between consonants. Almost all the medial clusters of Magahī are the best examples of it as we have already seen in the chapter 3.3. It may be illustrated as under :

(a) The syllable boundary takes place between such consonants which belong to the same type or position. For instance in /cək-ta/ 'spot' where both /k/ and /t/ are stops and in /əm-ba/ where /m/ and /b/ are bilabials.

(b) It may be found also between those consonants which have quite different classes, *i.e.*, /pər-ba/ 'the last performance', /məl-ka/ 'lightening', /məh-kəl/ 'smelt' where the first element of every word is trill, lateral, spirant and the second ones bilabial and velar stops respectively.

(c) In the case of intervocalic geminated consonants the syllable boundary falls within gemination, never before or after it. *e.g.*,

/cUl-lU/	'handful'
/pət-ta/	'leaf'
/bIc-ca/	'seed'

Regarding the three consonant clusters which have low frequency in the language the cut comes between their two elements. The syllable division may be found after first component within the three consonant clusters, *e.g.*,

/sən-tri/	'night guard'
/gen-dri/	'old and useless clothes'
/jən-mla/	'please take birth'
/pən-pnal/	'sharply'

Morpheme boundary very often decides the syllable boundary also. The syllable division usually comes within two morphemes.[4] *e.g.*,

/bIn-al/	'woven'
/lər̥ək-pən/	'childhood'
/gotI-arI/	'brotherhood'
/bəmta-ha/	'obstinate'

All the vowel sequences have a syllable boundary between the vowels. In the sequence of two vowels /vv/, the syllable division must appear in between them, *e.g.*,

/I-ad/	'memory'
/pU-ar/	'hay'
/pI-e/	'drink'
/dU-ari/	'door'

The syllable boundaries of the so-called sequence of three

and four vowels have already been examined (chap. 2.4). Some examples, however, are desirable here to show the cut as given below :

(a) /nəi-e/ 'boat'
/kəu-a/ 'crow'
/ji-əi/ 'live long'
/le-au/ 'bring'

(b) /khəi-əi/ 'would I eat?'
/chui-əu/ 'would I touch?'

General Remarks

There are more disyllabic words in the dialect than monosyllabic and trisyllabic words.

The syllable pattern of Magahī shows various types, however initial cluster never exists. The pattern of four and five syllables also may be observed, but they are few in number.

Magahī words may begin either with a consonant or a vowel but the number of such words which begin with consonants is more than those which have vowels initially.

Every word may begin with any vowel and consonant except /ṛ/, /w/ and /y/.

Almost all monosyllabic and disyllabic patterns have their nasalized forms also.

Word Structure

Different kinds of word-structures of Magahī are shown systematically in the following sub-section :

Monosyllabic Words

1. v	:	i	/i/	'this'
		u	/u/	'that'

			o	/o/	'a sort of exclamation'
			e	/e/	'a sort of address'
2.	v͜v	:	/a͜i/	'a sort of exclamation'	
			/o͜i/	'a sort of acceptance'	
			/ə͜u/	'and'	
			/a͜u/	'come', 'and'	
3.	vc	:	ə	/əb/	'now'
			U	/Ug/	'rise'
			a	/ag/	'fire'
			i	/id/	'a festival of Muslims'
			u	/un/	'wool'
			e	/ek/	'one'
			o	/ol/	'tuber'
4.	v͜vc	:	ə͜i	/ə͜ib/	'demerit'
			ə͜u	/ə͜ur/	'and'
5.	ṽc	:	ə̃	/ə̃ṛ/	'to insist'
			ã	/ãkh/	'eye'
			ũ	/ũṭ/	'camel'
			ẽ	/ẽṛ/	'heel'
			õ	/õs/	'dew'
6.	vcc	:	ə	/əng/	'organ'
			I	/Inc/	'inch'
			U	/Ucc/	'high'

7. cv	:	ə	/nə/	'no'
		i	/ki/	'what' or 'that'
		a	/kha/	'eat'
		i	/ghi/	'ghee'
		u	/cu/	'leak'
		e	/le/	'take'
		o	/dho/	'wash'
8. cy͜y	:	əi	/pə͜i/	'charge'
		ai	/ga͜i/	'cow'
		oi	/to͜i/	'lace'
		ui	/su͜i/	'needle'
		əu	/gə͜u/	'cow'
		au	/na͜u/	'put down'
		eu	/ne͜u/	'foundation'
		iu	/pi͜u/	'lover' or 'husband'
9. cṽ	:	ã	/hã/	'yes'
		ũ	/hũ/	'yes'
		ẽ	/dẽ/	'give'
		õ	/cõ/	'a sort of sound'
10. cvc	:	ə	/ghər/	'house'
		I	/ghIr/	'around'
		U	/bUl/	'walk'
		a	/dan/	'donation'
		i	/cij/	'thing'
		u	/phul/	'flower'

		e	/der/	'late'
		o	/mol/	'cost'
11. cv͜vc	:	ə͜i	/mə͜il/	'dirt'
		a͜i	/gha͜il/	'wounded'
		ə͜u	/mə͜uj/	'happiness'
		e͜u	/ne͜ur/	'mongoose'
		i͜u	/ki͜ul/	'the town of kiul'
12. cṽc	:	ə̃	/hə̃s/	'laugh'
		ũ	/sũt/	'sleep'
		ĩ	/hĩg/	'asafoetida'
		ã	/sãs/	'breath'
		ĩ	/khĩc/	'draw'
		ũ	/phũk/	'blow'
		ẽ	/phẽk/	'throw'
		õ	/sõs/	'crocadile'
13. cvcc	:	ə	/kənṭh/	'throat'
		I	/sIkkh/	'sikh'
		U	/lUnjh/	'paralysed'
		a	/kanh/	'a name of Lord Krishna'

Disyllabic Words

14. v-cv	:	ə	/əbhi/	'just now'

	a	i	e
ə	əgha 'satis-fied'	əji 'a sort of address'	əre 'a sort of address'

U		Uṭha 'please get up'	Uṭhi 'please get up'	Uge 'rise'
a	/abə/	'please come'	/ahu/	'please come'
	/ala/	'when you come'	/ari/	'saw'
	/are/	'far'	/ajo/	'come on'

15. vv-cv : əi̯ /əi̯la/ 'have you come?'

əu̯ /əu̯ra/ 'a sort of fruit'

oi̯ /oi̯na/ 'a name of a village'

16. ṽ-cv : /ãdhi/ 'storm'

17. v-cvc :

	ə	I	U
ə	ələg 'separate'	əgIn 'fire'	əhUṭh 'uncivilized'
I	Idhər 'here'	IdhIr 'on this side'	IjUn 'here'
U	Umər 'age'	UcIt 'right'	UjUr 'objection'
a	abəl 'being come'	akhIr 'end'	atUr 'impatient'
u	usər 'desert'		

	a	i	u	e	o
ə	əbaj 'sound'	əhir 'a caste'	əjur 'request'	əber 'early hour'	əhor 'request'
U	Ughar 'put off'		Ujur 'objection'	Uber 'clear weather'	

18. ṽ-cvc /ãdhər/ 'blind'
19. vc-cv ə /əkṛa/ 'rough rice'
I /Itna/ 'this much'
U /Unka/ 'his'
/UllU/ 'owl'
/Ubbe/ 'to be off'
/Ukṛu/ 'difficulty'
20. vc-cṽ /ejjã/ 'here'
21. vc-cvc

	ə	I	U
ə	ənkər 'of other'	əntIm 'last'	əjgUt 'wonderful'
I	Inkər 'his'	–	–
U	Umsəl 'much heated'	–	–

	a	u	o
ə	ənḍhar 'dark'	əmdur 'fruit'	–
I	Inkar 'refusal'	–	Injor 'light'
U	Utsah 'encouragement'	–	–

Contd...

22. v-vc	I	/Iad/	'memory'
23. v-cvc-c	ə	/əgəst/	'an English month'
	U	/Uṛənt/	'to flutter'
24. vc-cvc-c		/ərbInd/	'name of a boy'
25. ṽc-cv		/ ãcra/	'a part of sari'
26. ṽc-ccv	ə̃	/ə̃ngna/	'courtyard'
	ũ	/ũngli/	'finger'
27. cv-v	/rua/		'cotton'
	/roe/		'weep'
	/dio/		'would I give?'
	/chuə/		'please touch'
28. cv-ṽ	/bhuõ/		'even earth'
29. cv-cv			

	ə	/həba/	'air'
		/gərI/	'coconut'
I		/mIle/	'get'
U		/gUru/	'teacher'

a	i	u	e		o
a	kara 'black colou-red' (he)	kari 'black coloured' (she)	babu 'big boss'	bare 'sacri-fice'	Saro 'name of a girl'
i	nila 'a colour'	piri 'yellow'	sibu 'name of a boy'	tire 'side of river'	ghiyo 'even ghee'
u	buṛha 'old man'	suṛhi 'a caste'	huhu 'a sort of sound'	chuye 'touch'	duho 'to milk'
e	bela 'time'	teli 'oil man'	rehu 'a sort of fish'	ghere 'surround'	deho 'please give'

Contd...

Contd...

o	dhola 'please wash'	boli 'speech'	boku 'fool'	bole 'tell'	bole 'happeṇed'

30. cṽ-cṽ	/pãcõ/	'tive'
31. cv-cṽ	/kəhĩ/	'some where'
	/gehũ/	'wheat'
32. cṽ-cv	/hə̃si/	'laughter'
	/pãka/	'mud'
33. cv-cvc		

	ə	I	U
ə	nəsəl 'impure'	cərIt 'character'	cətUr 'wise'
I	bIgəṛ 'destroy'	–	bIgUl 'a sort of whistle, (bugle)'
U	hUnər 'art'	–	bUrus 'brush'
a	bapəs 'coming back'	bapIs 'coming back'	jamUn 'a sort of black fruit'
i	nipəl 'washed'	–	nihUr 'bent'
u	phuhər 'energetic' 'health'	dukhIt 'disturbed'	kUkUr 'dog'
e	sehət 'health'	–	–
o	dohər 'a thick wrapper'	rohIt 'a name'	gokUl 'a famous place'

	a	i	u	e	o
ə	səlam 'a sort of wish'	həkim 'doctor'	khəjur 'a sort of dry fruit'	bəreṛ 'cei-ling'	məror 'a kind of stomach pain'
I	nIlar 'fore-head'	—	—	—	bIyog 'separa-tion'
U	sUhag 'fortune'	—	—	—	sUjog 'Chance'

34. cv-cṽc /pəhŨc/ 'approach'
35. cṽ-cvc /sə̃bhal/ 'aware'
36. cv-vc /pUar/ 'hay'
/bIog/ 'separation'
/pIət/ 'drink'
37. cv-ṽc /kŨər/ 'lovely son'
38. cv-cvc-c /bəsənt/ 'spring'
/sUkhənt/ 'which is going to be dried'

39. cvc-cv

	a	i	u	e	o
ə	bədra 'cloud'	bəlki 'but'	səttu 'a sort of flour'	phətte 'a name'	gəccho 'accept'
I	hInkha 'his'	ḍhIlli 'loose'	hIndu 'a race'	hInkhe 'his'	tInko 'even piece'
U	kUrta 'a sort of cloth'	mUrti 'emage'	jUgnu 'night worm'	sUtle 'sleep'	sUtlo 'sleep'

	a	i	u	e
a	saṭna 'to paste'	padri 'christian missionary or priest'	phaltu 'extra' 'enough'	—
i	tisra 'third'	kimti 'costly'	sinthu 'name of a village'	nipte 'a sort of washing'
u	putna 'a name'	—	—	—
e	resma 'name of a girl'	resmi 'silken'	—	—
o	bolta 'soul'	bolti 'life'	—	—

40. cṽc-cv	/khə̃jri/	'a kind of musical instrument'
	/cãdni/	'moon light'
41. cvc-cṽ	/gellũ/	'would I suffer'
42. cvc-ccv	/jəntri/	'a sort of superstitious thing'

43. cvc-cvc :

	ə	I	U
ə	nəkkəl 'carica-ture'	pəcchIm 'west'	kəlchUl 'a kitchen implement'
i	hĨnkər 'his'	pInpIn 'weeping'	bIlkul 'complete'
U	bUṛbək 'fool'	—	dhUlmUl 'which is not fixed'
a	marphət 'through'	—	kanpUr 'Kanpur'
i	birbəl 'a name'	—	—
u	cumkər 'after kissing'	—	phulpUr 'name of a village'
e	jekkər 'of another man'	—	—
o	bhotthər 'which is not sharp'	—	—

	a	i	u	e	o
ə	bərsat 'rainy season'	nəmkin 'salty'	mənjur 'accept'	bənber 'a kind of fruit'	səntos 'satis-faction'
I	bIsbas 'faith'	—	tIrsul 'a sort of weapon'	sIgreṭ 'cigarette'	—
U	cUpcap 'silent'	—	—	—	—

44.	cvc-cvcc	/sətsəng/	'religious symposium'
45.	cvc-ccvc	/chəṭpṭal/	'suffered from pain'
46.	cv͜v-v	/kə͜ua/	'crow'
47.	cv-v͜v	/li͜əu/	'would I take?'
48.	cv͜v-v͜v	/khə͜iə͜i/	'would I eat?'

Trisyllabic Words

49.	v-cv-cv	/U-pa-dhi/	'degree'
50.	ṽ-cv-cv	/ə̃-dhe-ra/	'dark'
51.	v-cv-cvc	/ə-jə-gUt/	'wonderful'
52.	v-cvc-cv	/I-kəṭ-ṭhe/	'organised'
53.	v-cvc-cvcc	/ə-kəl-mənd/	'wise'
54.	vc-cvc-cv	/əs-mən-ma/	'sky'
55.	cv-cv-cv	/be-ləu-wa/	'name of a place'

	a	i	u	e	o
a	mə-ra-ṭha 'a resident of Mara-tha'	də-ma-hi 'a perfor-mance of agriculture'	tə-ra-ju 'scale'	sə-ra-he 'Praise'	də-ba-ho 'press'
i	mə-hi-na 'month'	—	—	—	mə-ni-no 'months'
u	nə-mu-na 'specimen'	—	—	—	nə-mu-no 'even a speciman'
e	—	bə-re-li 'a place'	gh-əre-lu 'domestic'	sə-be-re 'early in the morning'	—
o	mə-ho-ba 'a histo-rical place'	ni-go-ri 'a bad name'	—	bi-do-re 'disfigured'	—

56.	cv-cv-cṽ	/dU-nI-yã/	'world'
57.	cv-v-cv	/dU-ə-ri/	'door'
		/pI-ə-ri/	'yellow cloth'
58.	cv-cv-vc	/sə-sU-ar/	'father-in-law's house'
		/ci-cU-ai/	'sweating'
59.	cv-cv-cvc	/bI-ya-ban/	'deserted place'
		/jə-ba-hər/	'a kind of demon'
60.	cv-cvc-cvc	/sU-ren-dər/	'name of a boy'
		/pə-həl-ban/	'wrestler'
61.	cv-cvc-cv	/lə-ləc-te/	'with greed'
		/mə-hat-ma/	'saint'
62.	cv-cṽ-cvc	/jə-hã-gir/	'the mugal emperor Jahangir'
63.	cvc-cv-cv	/dər-ma-ha/	'monthly salary'
64.	cvc-cvc-cv	/bəs-phəṭ-ṭa/	'a thin and small form of bamboo'
65.	cvcc-cvc-cvc	/səng-mər-mər/	'marble'

With Four or More Syllables

66.	ṽ-cv-cv-cv	/Ĩ-jo-rI-ya/	'moon light'
67.	cv-cv-cv-cv	/bə-ra-bə-ri/	'similarity'
68.	cv-cv-vc-v	/hə-rI-ər-i/	'green-ness'
69.	cv͜v-cv-cv-cv	/cə͜u-kI-da-ri/	'the work of a night guard'
70.	cv-cv-v͜v-cv	/be-ṭI-ə͜u-ri/	'bride's troussers and other things'

71. cv-cv-cv-cvv /dI·ya·sə·lai/ 'match box'

72. cv-cvc-cv-cv-cv /kə-jər-hə-ṭI-ya/ 'a tribe'

FREQUENCY

Introductory

This study is intended to find out the relative frequency of segmental phonemes in running text. For the full characterisation of the phonological structure of a language it is desirable to have a reliable statistical information about the relative frequency of the phonemes.

The Nature of Texts

The whole statistical results which are given into two classified tables are based on ten running texts, transcribed phonemically into 3,155 words. It contains 11,383 phonemes. These texts are the colloquial narratives current in Nālandā, containing some conversations. Here these are given in App. I along with English translations. In these texts, there is no attempt to include the literary form of Magahī which is growing now. All care has been taken to present the colloquial form of the language as it is spoken by the best native speakers.

Procedure of Analysis

While collecting and analysing the data the following procedure was followed :

The word was assumed as a unit of collection. "By the term 'word' is meant any institutionalized word in the language, irrespective of its linguistic peculiarity".[5] Each word of these running texts at first is transcribed separately on a separate slip.

For the purpose of counting the occurrences of every individual phoneme a big table was prepared with different rows. One row was fixed for one phoneme. Every row was divided into three heads according to initial, medial and final occurrences of phonemes. After that, on the basis of every phonemically transcribed slip the occurrence of every phoneme was indicated on the table as a short mark according to its initial, medial and final position. Having prepared the full table of every occurrence in classified positions, a total counting was made at the end of every position. In this way every phoneme got its frequency in every position. The total frequency of a phoneme was the number of its occurrence in its different positions.

After getting the frequency of every phoneme, two tables were prepared. One of them was arranged in an alphabetical order showing the position-wise occurrences of phonemes and the second was arranged in descending order showing only its total frequency.

The two statistical tables in different order will help to draw a clearcut picture of the distributional character of individual phonemes.

Results and Conclusions

The frequency figures of the tables suggest some remarks which are stated below :

The relative frequency of voiceless : voiced, unaspirated : aspirated stops on the one hand and pure : diphs. vowels on the other hand yield an important result that the simpler phonemes have more frequency than the complex phonemes. It supports Zipf's principle, *i.e.*, simpler phonemes tend to be more frequent than more complex phonemes.[6] According to the frequency it may be presented as follows :

vl.	unasp. stops	:	1655
vd.	unasp. stops	:	1154
vl.	asp. stops	:	277
vd.	asp. stops	:	131
	Pure vowels	:	4797
	Diphs.	:	355

The liquids /l r/ are more frequent than spirants /s h/ and nasals /m n/, *i.e.*,

Liquids : 1323

Spirants : 712

Nasals : 701

Among consonants flap /ṛ/ and frictionless continuants /w y/ are less frequent. *e.g.*,

flap : 123

fric. conts : 155

Vowel phonemes have the highest frequency due to the fact that they can form a syllable by themselves with or without the consonants.

All long vowels are more frequent but the short vowel /ə/ is at the top.

Among diphs. /ə͜i a͜u ə͜u/ have a more common occurrence but /ə͜i/ is much more frequent. Of diphs. /e͜u/ and /i͜u/ did not show their occurrence at all even in the running texts of over 11,383 phonemes. It does not mean that they do not exist in the language. Owing to their restricted frequency they might be treated as marginal phonemes. Their examples can be found in chap. 2.3. /u͜i/ is also strikingly less frequent.

Almost all long and short vowels show most of their occurrences in their final and medial positions respectively.

Mostly consonants have the most common frequency in their initial positions except /t ṭ j ṭh n l r ṛ w y/. Of these /w y/ never occur initially and finally. Among consonants/ḍ ḍh/ are less frequent.

The two classified tables show the distributional nature of every segmental phonemes which follow :

Relative Frequency of Segmental Phonemes

Table 6 : Arranged in Alphabetical Order

Vowels

		Initial	*Medial*	*Final*		*Total*
ə	:	76	1424	33	=	1533
a	:	33	419	415	=	867
I	:	7	258	17	-	282
i	:	53	41	326	=	420
U	:	18	228	17	=	263
u	:	94	28	20	=	142
e	:	90	280	494	=	864
o	:	101	180	145	=	426
ə͜i	:	22	51	131	=	204
a͜i	:	—	2	20	=	22
o͜i	:	2	1	7	=	10
u͜i	:	—	1	—	=	1
ə͜u	:	10	23	15	=	48
a͜u	:	68	—	2	=	70
e͜u	:	—	—	—		—
i͜u	:	—	—	—		—

Consonants

		Initial	*Medial*	*Final*		*Total*
k	:	479	389	105	=	973
kh	:	42	65	39	=	146
g	:	106	138	10	=	254
gh	:	14	—	—	=	14
c	:	58	53	9	=	120
ch	:	21	20	8	=	49
j	:	109	142	25	=	276
jh	:	2	3	9	=	14

Contd...

Contd...

ṭ	:	17	42	9	—	68
ṭh	:	6	14	4	=	24
ḍ	:	8	—	—	=	8
ḍh	:	1	—	—	=	1
t	:	81	103	74	=	258
th	:	7	10	16	=	33
d	:	133	50	21	=	204
dh	:	12	11	2	=	25
n	:	95	188	135	=	418
p	:	128	103	5		236
ph	:	20	2	3	=	25
b	:	232	112	68	=	412
bh	:	60	12	5	=	77
m	:	144	106	33	=	283
y	:	—	93	—	=	93
r	:	192	288	251	=	731
ṛ	:	—	96	27	=	123
l	:	155	291	146	=	592
w	:	—	62	—	=	62
s	:	122	98	36	=	256
h	:	226	185	45	=	456

Relative Frequency of Segmental Phonemes

Table 7 : Arranged in the Descending Order

ə	:	1533	i	:	420
k	:	973	n	:	418
a	:	867	b	:	412
e	:	864	m	:	283
r	:	731	I	:	282
l	:	592	j	:	276
h	:	456	U	:	263
o	:	426	t	:	258
s	:	256	ə͜u	:	48

Contd...

Contd...

g	:	254	th	:	33
p	:	236	ph	:	25
ə͜i	:	204	dh	:	25
d	:	204	ṭh	:	24
kh	:	146	a͜i	:	22
ụ	:	142	jh	:	14
ṛ	:	123	gh	:	14
c	:	120	o͜i	:	10
y	:	93	ḍ	:	8
bh	:	77	ḍh	:	1
a͜u	:	70	ui	:	1
ṭ	:	68	eu	:	—
w	:	62	iu	:	—
ch	:	49			

REFERENCES

1. *An Outline of English Phonetics,* Daniel Jones, 1962, p. 55.
2. *Motor Phonetics,* R.H. Stetson, 1951, p. 29.
3. *Ibid.,* p. 27.
4. *Indian Linguistics,* Turner Jubilee Volume, 1959.
   Hindi Syllabic Structure, R.C. Mehrotra, p. 233.
5. *Phonemic and Morphemic Frequencies in Hindi,* A.M. Ghatage, 1964, p. iv.
6. *The Psychobiology of Language*, G.K. Zipf, 1936, pp. 68-81.

Section II

SUPRA-SEGMENTAL PHONEMES

6
NASALIZATION

Introductory

Nasalization of Magahī is a vocalic syllabic element occuring along with all vowels. It is here symbolized by / ˜/, placed over the vowels.

Contrast

All the vowels have their nasalized counter parts. Nasalized and non-nasalized vowels show phonemic contrast. *e.g.*,

Pure Vowels

/i/, / ĩ/

/dehi/	'body'	/dehĩ/	'give'
/gahi/	'a numeral'	/gahĩ/	'sing'

/I/, / Ĩ/

/ḍIg/	'slack'	/ḍĨg/	'bost'
/bIdh/	'rules regulations'	/bĨdh/	'a famous mountain'

/e/, /ẽ/

/bher/	'deep sleeping'	/bhẽr/	'sheep'
/ret/	'sand'	/rẽt/	'cut'

/ə/, /ə̃/

/əg/	'world'	/ə̃g/	'organ'

/pəkh/	'a fortnight'	/pə̃kh/	'feather'

/a/, /ã/

/bas/	'lodge'	/bãs/	'bamboo'
/aṭh/	'eight'	/ãṭh/	'stone of a fruit'

/o/, /õ/

/sos/	'to be ended'	/sõs/	'parpoise'
/oṭ/	'vote'	/õṭ/	'side'

/U/, /Ũ/

/balU/	'sand'	/balŨ/	'would I put on' (*e.g.* a lamp)
/ḍhəlUa/	'drunkard'	/ḍhəlŨa/	'slopy'

/u/, /ũ/

/cur/	'press'	/cũr/	'joint portion of a cot'
/lehu/	'blood'	/lehũ/	'I take'

Diphthongs

/ə͜i/, /ə͜ĩ/

/kə͜ia/	'moss'	/kə̃͜ia/	'miser'
/sə͜ia/	'bed'	/sə͜ĩa/	'lover'

/a͜i/, /a͜ĩ/

/ca͜i/	'tea'	/ca͜ĩ/	'seed'
/ba͜i/	'wind of stomach'	/ba͜ĩ/	'left'

/o͜i/, /o͜ĩ/

/ko͜ia/	'palm fruit'	/ko͜ĩa/	'a kind of vegetable'
/po͜ia/	'baby snake'	/po͜ĩa/	-do-

/u͜i/, /u͜ĩ/

/bu͜ia/	'a subject of fear'	/bhu͜ĩa/	'earth'

/ə͜u/, /ə͜ũ/

'gə͜ua/	'cow'	'gə̃͜ua/	'village'
/pə͜ua/	'a measurement'	/pə̃͜ua/	'feet'

/a͜u/, /ã͜u/

/ga͜u/	'sing'	/gã͜u/	'village'
/cha͜u/	'dramatic action'	/chã͜u/	'shade'

/e͜u/, /ẽ͜u/

/che͜u/	''hurdle'	/chẽ͜u/	'news of goodness'
/se͜u/	'apple'	/sẽ͜u/	'to serve'

/i͜u/, /ĩ͜u/

/pi͜u/	'lover'	/pĩ͜u/	'shall I drink'
/si͜u/	'Lord Śiva'	/sĩ͜u/	'would I stitch'

Kinds of Nasalization

The Magahī nasalization, at first, may be considered under two heads :

(a) Dependent nasalization and (b) Independent nasalization.[1]

(a) Dependent nasalization is a result of adjecent nasals and it is treated here as the phonetic features of nasal phonemes. It occurs either before or after the nasals.

(b) Independent nasalization always occurs as a spontaneous phenomena[2] which is free from the effect of nasal consonants.

Secondly, the degree of nasalization may be determined by the quantity of the vigorous lowering of the velum through which the air current passes.[3] It may be descriminated as (i) strong, (ii) medial and (iii) weak. Every degree has its own conditions which are accompanied by the two kinds of nasalization, mentioned above.

Independent Nasalization

The independent nasalization which is quite independent of nasal consonants, is always characterized by vowels either with the long ones like /i e a o u/ or with the short ones like /I ə U/. With short vowels it is always accompanied by the sonorous consonants like /r ṛ l s h y/.[4]

The degree of the nasalization of the two forms, mentioned above may be different from each other. The nasalization of long and short vowels in respect to the degree, may be recognised as strong and weak respectively.

From the view point of distribution the independent nasalization of strong degree occurs in every position. *e.g.*,

/ãc/	'fire'	/ãṛ/	'testicle'
/ĩṭ/	'brick'	/ũṭ/	'camel'
/kũs/	'a kind of hay'	/sõph/	'a kind of spice'
/bãjh/	'barren'	/sõs/	'parpoise'
/ghãs/	'grass'	/phãk/	'a piece of a fruit'
/garũ/	'would I squeeze	/bãḍhũ/	'would I bind'

Initially and finally the independent nasalization of week degree is followed and preceded by sonorous consonants respectively. *e.g.*,

Initial

/ə̃cra/	'a part of sari'	/ə̃ṛəl/	'stuck'
/Ũsau/	'a process of boiling'	/Ĩrot/	'side'
/Ũh/	'a sort of speech'	/ə̃sna/	'a month'

Final

/gahĨ/	'sing'	/əilə̃/	'have you come'
/sə̃ṛsĨ/	'tongs'	/becŨ/	'would I sell?'
/kəhŨ/	'would I tell?'	/kərhĨ/	'do'

Medially the nasalization of weak degree may occur either after or before the sonorous consonants. *e.g.*,

/ghŨs/	'take entrance'	/sə̃bə̃r/	'decorate'
/phə̃s/	'engage'	/kəhə̃r/	'sound of pain'
/sĨyar/	'fox'	/bĨhən/	'seeds'
/pə̃ṛkI/	'a kind of small bird'	/hĨrsa/	'competition'
/hĨya/	'here'	/sə̃sta/	'cheep'
/pə̃ləni/	'name of a village'	/phŨhĨ/	'raining in drops'

Allophonic Nature

The significant nasalization of Magahī can be considered as a phoneme and the two types of its as allophones. The two forms of independent nasalization which have their own conditions, can be treated as its allophones.

Dependent Nasalization

Dependent nasalization occurs initially, medially as well as finally. All the vowels of dependent nasalization consist of the medial degree. Initially and finally it is always followed or preceded by the nasals. *e.g.*,

Initial

[ə̃nəde·sa·]	/ənədesa/	'hope'
[ãm]	/am/	'mango'
[Ĩnk͜<ər]	/Inkər/	'his'
[Ũmr͜əl]	/Umr̤əl/	'flooded'
[o͜ĩna·]	/o͜ina/	'a name of a place'
[ə͜ĩma·]	/ə͜ima/	'would you come?'

Final

[ə͜ĩnə̃^·]	/ə͜inə/	'have you come?'
[dUnĩa·]	/dUnia/	'world'
[da·mĩ·]	/dami/	'costly'
[lə̃m͜nĩ·]	/ləmni/	'an earthen pot'
[lẽ·mũ·]	/lemu/	'lemon'
[nə͜ĩ]	/nə͜i/	'no'
[mə͜ĩa]	/mə͜ia/	'girl'

Medial

In the medial position it may be (a) followed or (b) preceded by the nasals, *e.g.*,

(a)	[dəhĩn]	/dəhin/	'kindful'
	[bImãn]	/bIman/	'airoplane'
	[bə>kə̯ĩn]	/bəkə̯in/	'old barren'
	[k<ə̃u̯n]	/kəun/	'who ?'
(b)	[k<əmə̃r]	/kəmər/	'waist'
	[mã·jəl]	/majəl/	'washed'
	[nĩmə̃>k]	/niɪnək/	'salt'
	[so·nãr]	/sonar/	'goldsmith'
	[mõm]	/mom/	'wax'
	[mə̯ĩnã·]	/mə̯ina/	'a kind of bird'
	[nĨar]	/nIar/	'presentation'

As far as Magahī is concerned, the rules regarding nasalization which have been suggested by B.N. Prasad are not applicable here.[5]

Morphemic Characteristics

Magahī nasalization has a special morphemic characteristic, that, the imperative verbs will be nasalized finally occuring without the sense of respect in the contrast of its counterparts. *e.g.*,

/khə̯ilə̃/	'tell me, have you taken your meal?'
/khə̯ilə/	'please tell me, have you taken your meal?'
/jahã/	'tell me, are you going?'
/jaha/	'please tell, are you going?'
/abahũ/	'I am coming'
/abahu/	'please tell me, would you come?'

Prosodic Features

Nasalization is one of the significant prosodic features of Magahī in favour of which the following points can be set up :

That all the nasalized vowels occur initially, medially as well as finally.

That nasalization runs through a single vowel including diphthongs also or a domain of sequence of vowels. There is no such example of the sequence of vowels which has partial nasalization. The sequence of vowels is either all nasalized or all oral. *e.g.*,

/gə̃ue/	'village'	/jə̃ua/	'twin'
/sə̃ĩa/	'lover'	'dhũia/	'smoke'
/laũ/	'would I bring it?'	/juãr/	'a sort of physical action'

Nasalization never occurs only with a single phoneme but it is the result of extracting nasal features from all the vowels.[6]

Owing to the prosodic quality the nasalized vowels are intended to be lengthend against their counterparts. Thus, it adds more sonority to the oral ones which may be felt easily in the process of utterance.

REFERENCES

1. *Nasalization in Hindi Literary Works*, S. Verma, Journal of Deptt. of Letters XVIII, p. 3.
2. Spontaneous Nasalization in the Indo-Aryan Lang., Grierson, *JRAS*, 1922, p. 381.
3. *General Phonetics,* Heffner, 1952, p. 113.
4. *Ibid,* p. 74.
5. "As all the vowels in Bhoj. can be nasalized, it will be noticed that generally it is with the vowels of long duration that the nasalization or the '*anunāsika*' occurs and the '*anusvāra*' or the nasal after sound of the class to which the following sound belong, occurs with the vowels of relatively short duration...... It may be of interest to note that the observations made here about Bhojapurī will be found

broadly applicable to the other eastern-speech-forms like Magahī, Maithlī and also to several of the Hindi dialects like Brajabhāṣā and others". *The Position of the Nasals in the Bhojpurī Phonological System : Indian Linguistics,* 1955-56, p. 195.

6. *Structural Linguistics,* Zillig S. Harris, 1947, p. 136.

7
JUNCTURE

The Nature of Transition

Juncture is a dimension of time. We may assume this phoneme wherever we find a pause. The juncture phenomenon of Magahī is characterised by the transition between successive syllables and stress contours. The transition between two successive syllables is found as follows :

(i) between two vowels v + v,
(ii) between a vowel and a consonant v + c,
(iii) between a diphthong and a consonant v͜v + c, and
(iv) between two consonants c + c.

Kinds of Juncture

There are two sorts of juncture which are called (a) close juncture and (b) open juncture.

(a) Close juncture [‿] is accompanied by muddy transition and has no phonemic status.[1] It is much more common than sharp transition and coincides with syllable division which never takes place in monosyllabic words.[2]
(b) Open juncture / + / which always comes medially as an internal phenomenon, contains sharp transition and has a distinctive distribution against its counterpart.

The terminal contours in respect to their pause, may be recognised as junctures but here they are not considered as junctures due to their intonational character. Hence, they are analysed in the chapter of Intonation.

Contrast

Contrast between the junctures is given below :

/pia/	[pi·‿a·]	'lover or husband'
/pi + a/	/'pi· + ˋa·]	'please drink'
/jia/	[ji‿a·]	'state of mind'
/ji + a/	['ji+ˋa·]	'live long'
/kimət/	[k<i‿mət]	'cost'
/ki+mət/	[ˋk<i·'mət]	'what's your view?'
/khala/	[kha‿la·]	'mother's sister'
/kha+la/	['kha· +ˋla·]	'please eat'
/koi̯la/	[koi̯‿la.]	'coal'
[koi̯+la/	[ˋkoi̯+ˋla·]	'take any one'
/kəi̯las/	[k<əi̯‿las]	'a name'
/kəi̯+las/	[ˋk<əi̯+ˋlas]	'how many dead bodies?'
/gIrja/	[g<Ir‿ja·]	'name of a girl'
/gIr+ja/	[ˋg<ĭr+ˋja·]	'fall down'
/cəlna/	[cəl‿na·]	'to go'
/cəl+na/	[ˋcəl+ˋna·]	'don't go'

Phonetic Features

Magahī junctures are always accompanied by stress. Though stress is not significant in the dialect however, it plays an important role in the formation of juncture. Usually stress can be recognised as strong and weak of which weak is negligible to a great extent. On the other hand strong stress provides a clue to interprete a / + / which always occurs in between two strong stress contours. Due to its relative quantity strong stress may be descriminated as strong and stronger which are transcribed before strong stressed syllable by ['], ['] respectively.

Stress in Different Environments

The / + / always takes place either between two strong stress or between a strong and a stronger stress or vice versa. In different environments the stress patterns show their different kinds which are illustrated below :

In /v + c/ and /v͜v + c/ type junctures strong stress falls on both sides, *i.e.*, in pre-pausal position on initial sound and in post-pausal position on first consonant. *e.g.*,

/v + c/

/dukan/	[du‿kan]	'shop'
/du+kan/	[ˈdu+ˈkan]	'two ears'
/khaja/	[kha‿ja·]	'a kind of sweet'
/kha+ja/	[ˈkha+ˈja·]	'please eat'
/kimət/	[k<i‿mət]	'cost'
/ki+mət/	[ˈk<i+ˈmət]	'what's your view?'
/aja/	[a‿ja·]	'come on'
/a+ja/	[ˈa.+ˈja.]	'come and go'

/v͜v + c/

/kə͜ilas/	[kə͜i̯‿las]	'a name'
/kə͜i+las/	[ˈkə͜i̯+ˈlas]	'how many dead bodies?'

/koi̯la/	[koi̯‿la·]	'coal'
/koi̯+·la/	[ˋkoi̯+ˋla·]	'take any one'
/gəu̯na/	[g˂əu̯‿na·]	'second marriage'
/gəu̯+na/	[ˋgəu̯+ˋna·]	'not cow'

Such junctures which are of /v + v/ type, bear stronger stress on post-pausal vowels and strong stress on pre-pausal consonants. *e.g.*,

/jia/	[ji‿a·]	'state of mind'
/ji+a/	[ˋji.+ˋa·]	'live long'
/koi̯a/	[koi̯‿a·]	'inner part of palm fruit'
/koi̯+a/	[ˋkoi̯+ˋa.]	'any one come'
/pia/	[pi‿a·]	'lover or husband'
/pi+a/	[ˋpi+ˋa·]	'please drink'

In /c + c/ type junctures stress falls on the first consonants of both sides as stronger and strong respectively. *e.g.*,

/chəlke/	[chəl‿k˂e·]	'over lapping of water'
/chəl+ke/	[ˋchəlˋk˂e.]	'having deceived'
/kərja/	[k˂ər‿ja·]	'loan'
/kər+ja/	[ˋk˂ər+ˋja·]	'do something'
/ṭəpke/	[ṭəp‿k˂e·]	'to fall'
/ṭəp+ke/	['ṭəp+ˋk˂e·]	'after crossing'
/ṭhənke/	[ṭhən‿k˂e·]	'to thunder'

/ṭhən+ke/ [ˈṭhən+ˈk<e·] 'with full speed'

As far as my data is concerned there is no example of c + v type juncture in Magahī.

Junctures as Morphological Boundaries

Magahī / + / always breaks a macrosegment within its morphologic boundaries. It is most important thing in respect to juncture.[3] For an example /du + kan/ 'two ears' and /'kəi + las/ 'how many dead bodies?' are broken by the phoneme within two morphemes which determine their boundaries. Each of the junctures can be interpreted on this principle.

Though the analysis of Morphologic boundaries is beyond the consideration of phonology, however, it has been pointed out owing to the following reasons :

First, the phonemes of a language should be analysed without reference to morphology as I have done in this chapter.

Second, the phonetic features of morphologic boundaries can only be described by the assumption of juncture.[4]

REFERENCES

1. *A Course in Modern Linguistics*, Hockett, 1958, p. 55.
2. *Ibid., See Chap. 4.*
3. *Structural Linguistics,* Zellig S. Harris, 1961, p. 87.
4. *Juncture in Modern Standard German,* William G. Moulton, (Readings in Linguistics), 1957, p. 214.

8
INTONATION

Basic Elements

In this chapter an attempt is made to analyse the intonational structure of Magahī, constituted by (1). physical properties, (2). perceptible qualities, (3). linguistic meanings, (4). sense content and (5). the communicative "in woven nature" of speech intonation.[1]

Magahī intonation is described in terms of four pitch levels and two terminal contours. All the P.Ls. and T.Cs. are arranged in incrimental order and are relative to one another.

Four Pitch Levels

The four relative pitch levels are indicated by /1 2 3 4/. The pitch /1/ is low and /3/ is high, but /2/ is mid in between the two P.Ls., mentioned above. The /4/ is extra high.

Two Terminal Contours

The two T.Cs. are symbolized by /↓↑/falling and rising respectively. The terminal fall which is assigned to /↓/, consists of the retardation of tempo, accompanied by gradual ceasing of phonation. The terminal rise which is assigned to /↑ / is defined as sharp rise of phonation.

Contrast

The contrast among the four P.Ls. /1 2 3 4/ and two T.Cs. /↓↑/ shows their phonemic status as it is given below :

Table 8 : Analysis of Basic Elements

No.	*Phrase with Phonemic writing*	*Lexical meaning*	*Communicative Context*	*Explanation*	*Linguistic meaning*
1	2	3	4	5	6
1. (a)	/^{2}əccha^{2}↓/	O.K.	Ram : /əb tu ghər jo/ (now you go home) Shyam : /^{2}əccha^{2}↓/ (O.K.)	Being got an order if a Person says /^{2}əccha^{2}↓/ showing his **acceptance.**	narrative
(b)	/^{2}əccha^{3}↓/	-do-	Ram : /mohan ke bhed khUle pər səb bhənḍa phUt geləi/ (after disclosing the secret of Mohan all things appeared evidently) Shyam : /^{1}əccha^{3}/	Geting the meaning of a secrecy if one says it showing his **understanding**	hortatory
(c)	/^{1}əccha^{2}↑/	-do-	Ram :/ek dIn tor həm hUlIya ṭait kər de bəu/ (One day I shall beat you)	after a threat if a man meets the **challenge**.	-do-
(d)	/^{3}əccha^{1}↑/	O.K.	Ram : /u ki bol ləu ^{2}əccha^{1}↑/ (what did he say, well?)	**when some one asks** about the reply of another man	interrogative

Contd...

Contd...

(e)	/³əccha⁴↑/	-do-	Ram : /u sāp car mən ke ƚolə͜i/ (the weight of the snake was four mond (a kind of measurement). Shyam : /³əccha⁴↑/	when a person expresses his **surprise** about a wonderful matter.	exclamatory
2.(a)	/²hã¹↓/	Yes	Ram : /tu ghər jahĩ/ (do you go home?) Shyam : /²hã¹↓/ (yes)	when a man expresses his **acceptance**	narrative
(b)	/²hã²↓/	-do-	Ram : /okra abe pər həm i bat səmjh lũ ki u etna bId man ədmi he/ (after his meeting I felt he is a great scholar) Shyam : /²hã²↓/	getting the meaning of a secrecy while one shows his **understanding**	hortatory
(c)	/²hã²↑/	yes	Ram : /u ki kəhəl kəu, ²hã²↑/ (what did he say, yes?)	**If one asks a** person about the reply of another man.	interrogative
(d)	/⁴ hã⁴↑/	-do-	Ram : /ərjUn ke nIsana etna pəkka nIkəl lə͜i ki u sidhe cIṛIyã ke ãkh me jake ləg lə͜i/ (The aim of Arjun was so accurate that went directly to the eyes of the bird) Shyam : /⁴hã⁴↑/	**Being astonished,** if some one says like this	exclamatory

Contd...

Contd...

3.(a)	/^{2}jahĩ^{2}↓/'	go'	Ram says to Shyam : /tu ghər ^{2}jahĩ^{2}↓/ (you go home)	When a person **orders** another one for going any where.	hortatory
(b)	/^{2}jahĩ^{3}↓/	-do-	Ram asks Shyam : /u ki kəhəl kəu ^{2}jahĩ^{3}↓/ (what did he say, 'go'?)	When **some one asks** a person about the reply of another one	interrogative
(c)	/^{2}jahĩ^{4}↑/	go	Ram asks Shyam :/u ghər me ag ləg jai pər bhi u bol ləu ^{2}jahĩ^{4}↑/ (after to be fired the home, did he say go?)	**Being astonished** while a person asks	exclamatory
4.(a)	/^{2}həm^{2}↓/	myself	Ram :/i kam ke kər təi/ (who shall do this work ?) Shyam : /^{2}həm^{2}↓/ (myself)	While a person shows his **acceptance**	narrative
(b)	/^{3}həm^{3}↓/	-do-	Ram asks Shyam : /u ki kəhəl kəu ^{3}həm^{3}↓/ (what did he say, 'həm'?)	While a person asks about another man's reply	interrogative
(c)	/^{4}həm^{1}↑/	-do-	Ram : /etna bhari kam se bhi u nəi ḍər ləi/ (he did not get fear with such terrible work) Shyam : /au ki bol ləi ^{4}həm^{2}↑/ (and what did he say, 'həm'?)	With **wonder** while one asks about another man's reply	exclamatory
5.(a)	/^{2}həm ^{3}roṭi	I would	/u bol ləi ki ^{2}həm ^{3}roṭi kham^{3}↓/	**acceptance**	narrative

Contd...

Contd...

	kham^{3}↓/	eat bread	(he told that I shall eat bread)		
(b)	/^{2}həm roṭi ^{2}kham^{2}↑/	-do-	/u ki kəhəl kəu ki ^{2}həm roṭi ^{2}kham^{2}↑/ (what did he say that I shall eat bread)	**question**	interrogative
(c)	/^{2}həm ^{1}roṭi kham^{1}↓/	I would eat bread	/au koi dosər ədmi nəi bəlIk ^{2}həm roṭi ^{2}kham^{2}/_ (no one else but I will **eat bread)**	only I will eat bread no one else. **stress on 'həm'.**	hortatory
(d)	/^{1}həm roṭi ^{2}kham^{2}↓/	-do-	/jərur jərur ke ^{1}həm roṭi ^{2}kham^{2}↓/ (certainly I will eat bread)	Surely I will eat bread. **Stress on 'kham'**	-do-
(e)	/^{2}həm ^{4}roṭi kham^{2}↑/	-do-	/ḍaktər sahəb ki kəhəl thIn, ^{2}həm ^{4}roṭi^{2} kham^{2}↑/ (what did the doctor say, would I take bread?)	With **wonder** if one asks would I eat bread	exclamatory
6.(a)	/^{1}bIyana^{2} ^{2}del kəi^{1}↓/	he gave him advance money	/i bat pər okəra u ^{1}bIyana^{2} d^{2}el kəi^{1}↓/ (on this matter he gave him advance money)	**statement**	narrative
(b)	/^{2}bIyana ^{3}del kəi^{2}/_	-do-	/ki u ^{2}bIyana ^{3}del kəi^{2}↑/ (did he give him advance money?)	**question**	interrogative
(c)	/^{2}bIyana^{3} ^{4}del.kəi^{3}↑/	-do-	/i haləṭ pər bhi u okəra ^{2}bIyana^{3} ^{4}del kəi^{3}↑/ (on this serious condition did he give him advance money?	Realy did he give him advance money? **wonder**	exclamatory

Contd...

Contd...

			advance money?		
7.(a)	/^{1}tu ^{2}ghər jo^1↓/	you go home	/ram shyam se kəhəl kəi ki ^{1}tu ^{2}ghər jo^1↓/ (Ram said to Syam that you go to home)	**order**	narrative
(b)	/^{2}tu ^{3}ghər jo^1↑/	-do-	/u ki kəhəl kəu ki ^{2}tu ^{3}ghər jo^1↑/ (what did he say, you go home?)	**question**	interrogative
(c)	/^{2}tu ghər^4 jo^2↑/	-do-	/əisən halət pər bhi u bol ləu ^{2}tu ^{4}ghər jo^2↑/ (on this serious condition did he say, you go home?)	**wonder**	exclamatory
(d)	/^{2}tu ^{1}ghər jo^1↓/	-do-	/au koi nəi khali ^{2}tu ^{1}ghər jo^1↓/ (only you go home no body else)	**stress on 'tu'**	hortatory
(e)	/^{1}tu ghər^2 jo^2↓/	-do-	/IdhIr UdhIr nəi khali ^{1}tu ^{2}ghər jo^2↓/ (you go only home not elsewhere)	**stress on 'ghər'**	-do-
8.(a)	/^{2}gai nəi bəil^1↓/	neither cow nor ox	/okəra kUch nəi cahi, ^{2}gai nəi bəil^1↓/ (he does not wnat any thing neither cow nor ox)	**statement**	narrative
(b)	/^{1}gai nəi ^{2}bəil^1↑/	-do-	/i jənabər ki həi, nəi ^{1}gai	**question**	interrogative

Contd...

Contd...

			nəi ^{2}bəil^{1}↑/ (what is this animal, neither cow nor ox?), (whether this animal is neither cow nor ox?)		
(c)	/^{1}gai ^{2}nəi^{1}↓ ^{2}bəil^{1}↑/	-do-	/i ^{1}gai ^{2}nəi^{1} ^{2}bəil həi^{1}↑/ (it is not cow, but ox?)	**question**	-do-
(d)	/^{1}gai ^{4}nəi^{2}↑ ^{2}bəil^{1}↓/	-do-	/i ^{1}gai ^{4}nəi^{2}↑ ^{2}bəil həi^{1}↓/ (is it not cow but ox?)	**question**	-do-
9.(a)	/^{3}bəṛkI^{2} nəi ^{2}choṭki^{2}↓/	neither elder nor younger girl	/koi nəi mII ləi ^{3}bəṛkI nəi ^{2}choṭkI^{2}↓/ (no one could meet neither? elder nor younger girl)	**statement**	narrative
(b)	/^{1}bəṛkI^{2}nəi ^{2}choṭki^{1}↑/	-do-	/koi nəi həi ^{1}bəṛkI nəi ^{2}choṭkI^{1}↑/ (whether no one is there either elder or younger	**question**	interrogative
(c)	/^{2}bəṛkI ^{3}nəi^{1}↓ ^{3}choṭkI^{2}↑/	neither elder nor younger girl	/h^{2}uã ^{2}bəṛkI ^{3}nəi^{1}↓ ^{3}chotkI həi^{2}↑ (nor elder but younger girl is there ?)	**question**	interrogative
(d)	/^{1}bəṛkI ^{1}nəi^{2}↑ ^{3}chotkI^{1}↓/	-do-	/huã ^{1}bəṛkI ^{2}nəi^{2}↑ ^{2}choṭkI həi^{1}↓/ (is there not elder but	**question**	-do-

Contd...

Contd...

		younger?)		
10.(a) /^{2}khəi təi nə ^{2}pi təi^1↓/	he will neither eat nor drink	/u kUccho nəi kər təi, ^{2}khəi təi nə ^{2}pi təi^1↓/ (he will not do anything neither eat nor drink)	**statement**	narrative
(b) /^{2}khəi təi nə pi^3 təi^2↑/	-do-	/ki u ^{2}khəi təi nə ^{3}pi təi^2↑/ (will he not eat or drink?)	**question**	interrogative
(c) /^{3}khəi təi^2 nə^2↑/ ^{2}pi təi^1↓/	-do-	/ki u ^{3}khəi ^{2}təi nə^2↑ ^{2}khali pi təi^1↓/	**question**	-do-
(d) /^{2}khəi təi ^{3}nə^1↓ ^{2}pi təi^1↑/	-do-	(will he not eat but drink?) /u^2 khəi təi ^{3}nə^1↓ ^{2}kebəl pi	**question**	
11.(a) /^{1}u ja ^{2}həi^1↓/	he goes	/ram syam ke bare me bol/ ləi ki ^{1}u ja ^{2}həi^1↓/ (Ram told about Shyam that he goes)	**statement**	narrative
(b) /^{2}u ja ^{3}həi^1↑/	-do-	/ram ki kəhəl kəi ki u^2 ja ^{3}həi^1↑/ (what did Ram ask, is he going?)	**question**	interrogative
(c) /^{2}u ja ^{4}həi^2 ↑/	-do-	səce me u^2 ja nəi↑/	**wonder**	exclamatory
(d) /^{3}u ja ^{4}həi^2↓/	-do-	/au koi nəi u^3 ja həi^2↓/ (no body else, only he goes)	**stress on 'u'**	hortatory
(e) /^{2}u ^{3}ja ^{4}həi^2↓/	-do-	/əb to ^{2}u ja^3 həi^2↓/ (now he will surely go)	**stress on 'ja'**	-do-

Analysis of Basic Elements

All the examples mentioned above in a table do not show only contrast between P.Ls. and T.Cs. but provide also some more important features of intonation i.e., lexical meaning, communicative context, explanation and linguistic meaning.

All given examples are conditioned by their communicative context means that is "woven into" communicative situation. For this reason these are cited with their contexts and conversations and are supplimented by explanations.

Maghai intonation bears in itself the linguistic meaning without which we cannot perceive it adequately. The different types of Magahi intonation may be categorized in tetms of (i) narrative, (ii) interrogative, (iii) hortatory and (iv) exclamatory which are mentioned above their examples. Linguistic meaning is based on the system of lexical, grammatical and stylistic meanings and that is contrastive from other intonational meaning of the language.

The communicative types and the linguistic meanings of intonation express the sense contents of phrases. As a matter of fact, speech intonation conveys information not only about thoughts but also about the feelings and the will. It consists of the communicative levels and the speaker's attitude to the subjects.

As an instance a phrase /^{2}əccha^2↓/ contains five meanings which reveal different ideas of Magahī speaker. The different sorts of examples consist of different sorts of contents.

The perceptable qualities and physical properties determine the significant phonemic features of intonation *i.e.*, the four pitch levels /1, 2, 3, 4/ and the two terminal contours /↓↑/ which are conditioned by the frequency of vocal cord vibrations, duration, intensity and harmony.

The perceptable qualities of Magahī-intonation constitute a structural unity which is interwoven by stress, rhythm, tempo and duration. Rhythm makes a harmony within a macrosegment.

The physical properties are only a code which serves to transmit a system of linguistic meanings. The primary physical properties of Magahī are its frequency c/s, its intensity and time. These are interdependent and on every occasion form a particular structure.

Stress

Stress which is considered as breath-force has been described in terms of strong and weak in the chap. of juncture. Stress coincides with pitch levels. Often it is so difficult to decide whether stress or pitch or a combination of the two is responsible for a certain effect.[2] In colourless speech usually /3 4/ or /2/ bear strong stress and the rest one/1/ has weak stress. One macrosegment has only one strong stress. Such strong stressed position is called centre of a microsegment. From the center to the end of a macrosegment is recognised as head and the rest of it as pendent.[3] No macrosegment of Magahī can exist without head. *e.g.*,

/^{1}tu ^{2}ghər jo^1↓/ 'you go home'

In the above mentioned example /^{2}ghər/ is the centre on which strong stress falls. From /^{2}ghər/ to /jo^1/ is head of the phrase and the remaining part /^{1}tu/, low in pitch with weak stress, is pendent. The falling terminal contour /↓/ shows the gradual ceasing of phonation.

Distributional Positions

There are only four distributional positions in which the levels of pitch occur in contrastive variations : (i) immediately after terminal contour *i.e.*, simultaneous with the first syllable of the phrase, (ii) immediately before terminal contour, (iii) at strong stressed syllable and (iv) at weak stressed syllable.

A pitch phoneme has a segmental area from the point of its initiation up to the point where the next pitch phoneme is initiated. But this is not pertinent in case of last pitch phoneme before a terminal contour occupies only the area of its accurate phonetic occurrence.

Division of a Macrosegment

Whenever either a strong stressed P.L. or a T.C. occures within a span, the macrosegment may be divided into two parts. The T.Cs. usually break sentence contours. The various contour possibilities are four in number, *i.e.*, falling, rising, rising falling and falling rising. These are illustrated below :

/^{3}bəṛkI nə͜i ^{2}choṭkI^{2}↓/	'neither elder nor younger'
/^{1}bəṛkI nə͜i ^{2}choṭkI^{1}↑/	'whether no one is there either elder or younger?'
/^{2}bəṛkI ^{3}nə͜i^{1}↓ ^{3}choṭkI^{1}↑/	'not elder but younger?'
/^{1}bəṛkI ^{2}nə͜i^{2}↑ ^{3}choṭkI^{1}↓/	'is there not elder but younger?'

On the other hand a sentence may be divided into two parts if a strong stressed P.L. falls within a span. *e.g.*,

/^{1}həm roṭi ^{2}kham^{2}↑/ 'would I take bread?'

In above sentence /^{2}kham^{2}↑/, the strong stressed syllable, is the center and rest of it is pendent. So, the sentence automatically, can be divided into two parts as it is described above.

Now, on the basis of acoustic analysis we will try to ascertain the physical properties and perceptable qualities of the four P.Ls. and the two T.Cs.

Acoustic Analysis

Survey of Wave-forms

A wave-form is an integeral unit of a speech, which may be continuous and discontinuous also.[4] It is desirable in acoustic analysis of the intonation structure of a language, to make a rapid survey of the whole wave-form which displays the nature of the glottal puff during the utterence.

Of various examples, given in the table 8, some can be set up as the norms which present the complete nature of the intonation structure of Magahī /əccha/ and /hem roṭi kham/ are considered here under this assumption. The speech-records of these phrases are the representative ones which have been taken after a number of experiments on kymograph.

Though it is very difficult to assign the limits of individual speech in the path of a wave-form, however, an attempt is made to recognise the change-points, that is, of course, arbitrary.

The Wave-form of /²əccha² ↓/

At first the record of a short Magahī phrase /²əccha²↓/ which is exhibited over a base line, is studied here.

The record starts with a number of strong vibrations of high amplitudes and ascends in its middle portion. It ends at the droping down of the vibrations of small amplitudes which seem to suggest the weak nature of the intensity of the sound. This wave-bit is assigned to /ə/.

From the descending part of the initial speech the path of the wave-form presents a horizental line up to the sudden rise, showing the unreleased form of [c'], that is imperceptable also. The sudden rise in the path of the wave-form indicates the released breath-force of /ch/.

A number of strong vibrations are noticed with small amplitudes which indicate the beginning of /a/, the last speech of the wave-form. Medially it goes to high along with greater amplitudes and ends with weak vibrations.

Having a few continuous vibrations together with high amplitudes the wave-form fades away. It is followed by very weak vibrations. This wave-profile presents the nature of falling T.C. /↓/.

Looking at the whole curve, it is obvious that the whole utterance is made in one breath which is continuous one.

It is a general description of the wave-form of /əccha/. Owing to the different P.Ls. and T.Cs. the frequency of vibrations and the intensity (amplitudes) differs from each other. It is to be noticed that the different wave-forms are the results of the different P.Ls. and T.Cs.

The wave-form of /²həm ³roṭi kham³ ↓/

Let us proceed to survey another wave-form /²həm ³roṭi kham³↓/ which is quite different from the previous one. The whole wave-form is exhibited over a base-line which begins with an ascent, that is, due to the breath force of /h/. A range of stronger vibrations with higher amplitudes takes place from the decaying part of /h/. This wave-bit determines the speech form of /ə/. After the weak vibrations of the last portion of /ə/, a weaker vibrating body is seen displaying the occurance of /m/.

An abrupt jerk together with few vibrations, takes place in the path of the wave-form, showing the physical properties of /r̥/.

When consonants or vowels occur adjacently also the change-point is quite recognisable—in such a speech-record the change-point can be located with an appreciable accuracy. But, in such case, the change from one segment to another is not smooth.[5]

Afterwards a few strong vibrations with a few greater amplitudes are found. It is corresponded by some weak vibrations, indicating its decay. It is assigned to the speech-form of /o/. The path of wave, then, gets sudden rise with close vibrations and greater amplitudes. The sudden rise in the path of the wave-form is observed here owing to the breath force of /ṭ/ followed by the corresponding stronger vibrations of /i/. This wave-structure goes in a down straight path of the wave-form having considerable duration. Again the sudden rise, corresponded by the stronger continuous vibrations indicate the breath-force of /kh/ and the vibrations of /a/ respectively.

After a gradual periodic decay again a big jerk is observed getting some weaker vibrations, which decide the wave-bit of /m/. From the descending part of it the structure of falling T.C. starts, that is, described in preceding lines.

It is to be noticed in the preceding examples that a consonants and a vowel or a vowel and a consonant (c v or v c) while come together in speech, the change-point from the consonant to the vowel is not definite. Physico-phonetically vowels and consonants are mutually exclusive.[6]

Specific Character of P.Ls. and T.Cs.

Now, we will proceed to determine the specific character of the four P.Ls. and the two T.Cs. on which the intonation structure of Magahī is based.

Pitch is interpreted in terms of frequency of vibrations. The greater the frequency the higher is the tone and conversely. Intensity, that is sound energy is interpreted in terms of amplitude.

The two speech-forms which are assumed as representative records provide some clue in their different forms. In different environments and positions the four P.Ls. /1 2 3 4/ and the two T.Cs. /↓↑/ form their specific character according to their frequency c/s. After making a general survey of the frequency c/s of every intonation phoneme, it is found that every P.L. and T.C. is similar to a great extent. The average outlines, therefore, of every P.L. and T.C. are drawn in fig. 1, 2 and 3. This study is appedned also by the various speech records of /jahī/ and /bəṛki nəi choṭki/.

Figs. 1, 2 and 3 present the nature of every P.L. & T.C. The nature of the four P.Ls. /1 2 3 4/ is shown in fig. 1.

Description of P.Ls.

Their description follows :

/1/ is the lowest P.L. of Magahī which occurs in every position of a speech-form. It shows its highest frequency 200 c/s and lowest 160 c/s.

/2/ is the medial P.L. of Magahī, occurs in every position of a speech-form. Its frequency–range is as follows : 201-250 c/s.

/3/ is the highest P.L. of the language occuring initially, medially as well as finally.

The frequency-range is 251-275 c/s.

/4/ is the extra high P.L. of Magahī occurs mostly in the final position of a speech-form indicating exclamation. It shows higher intensity (amplitudes) than other P.Ls.

The frequency-range is as follows : 276-292-300 c/s.

The duration and intensity of every P.L is varied from one another. They are arranged in incrimental order. If /1/ bears longer duration and lowest intensity /3/, then, contains short duration and high intensity. /2/ lies in between the two P.Ls.

mentioned above. But /4/, *i.e.* extra high P.L. consists of shorter duration and highest intensity as it is evident from its frequency-range, *i.e.*, 276-292-300 c/s.

Description of T.Cs.

The two terminal contours *i.e.*, /↓↑/ are also arranged in incrimental order and are relative to one another.

/↓/, the falling T.C. begins at higher value at about not more than 245 c/s, falls gradually together with considerable duration.

/↑/, the rising T.C. begins with weak vibrations and low amplitudes and then rises to its maximum.

Frequency-range : 215-340 c/s.

On the basis of duration and intensity the two T.Cs. /↓↑/ differ from each other. If /↓/ is the maximum in its duration, on the other hand, /↑/ shows short duration and greater intensity.

REFERENCES

1. *Tone and Intonation*, Vladimir Artemov.
   Proceedings of the fourth International Congress of Phonetic Sciences, Helsinki, 1961, pp. 403-406.
2. *A Hand Book of English Intonation*, Armstrong and Ida C. Ward, 1955, p. 3.
3. A Course in Modern Linguistics : Hockett, 1958, p. 38.
4. *Researches in Experimental Phonetics,* E.W. Scripture, p. 25.
5. (a) *Phonemics of Old Tamil,* C.R. Sankaran, Poona, 1951, p. 39.
   (b) *Process of Speech,* C.R. Sankaran, Poona, 1963, p. 24.
   (c) *The utterance-continum and the a Phoneme,* C.R. Sankaran and S. Sourirajan, Bulletin of Deccan College, Poona, Vol. V, Nos. 1-2, pp. 5-15.
6. *A Study of the Japanese Phonemes* by Means of Tone Films. (Proc. of the 2nd International Congress of Phonetic Science, 1936), p. 119.

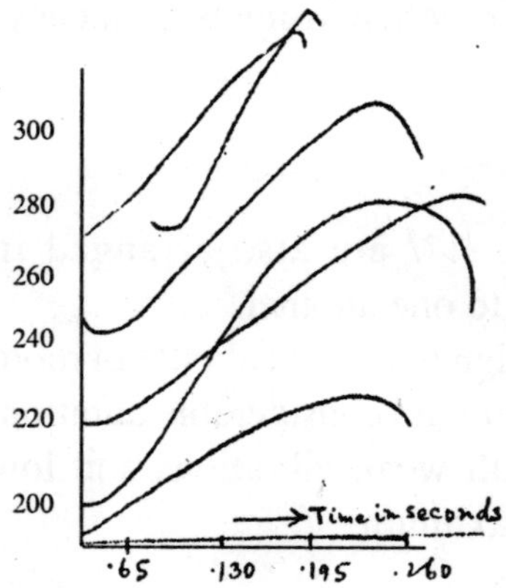

Fig. 1 : The Nature of Rising T.Cs.

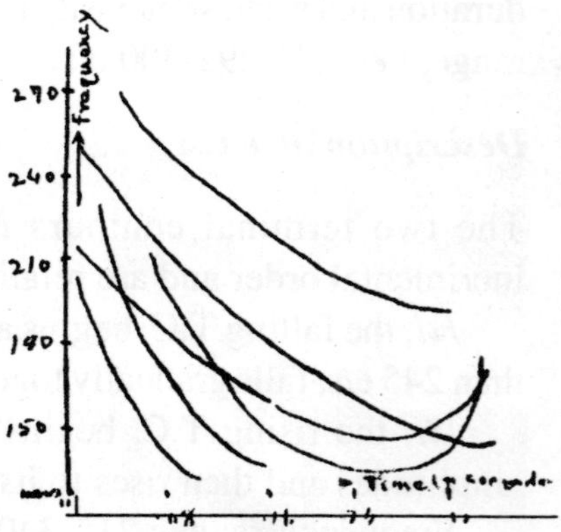

Fig. 2 : The Nature of Falling T.Cs.

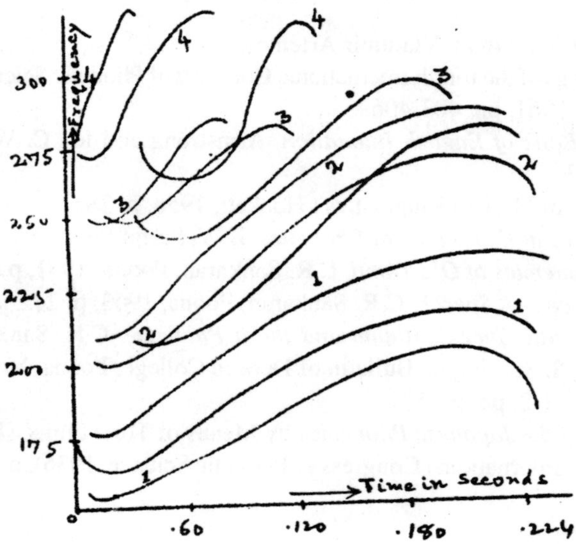

Fig. 3 : The Nature of four P.Ls.

Wave Forms

/əccha/

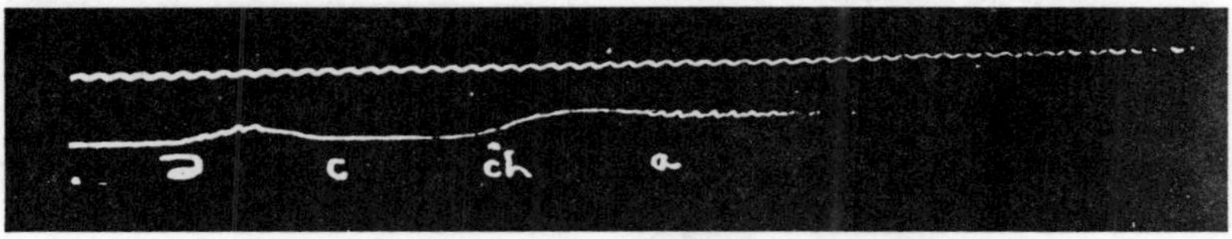

a

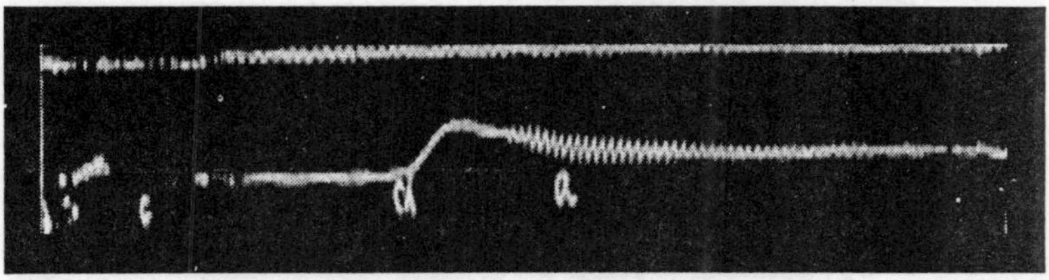

b

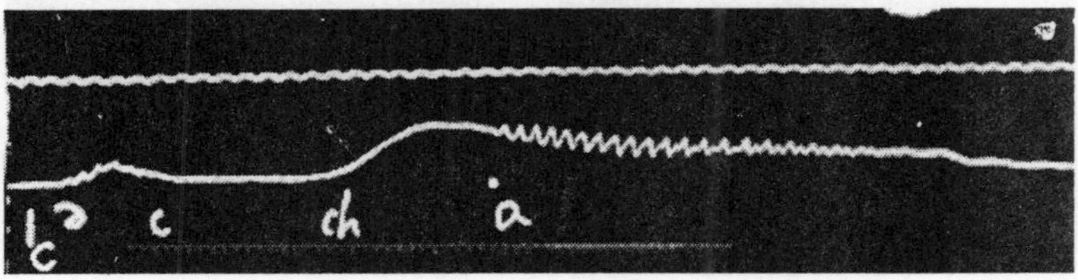

c

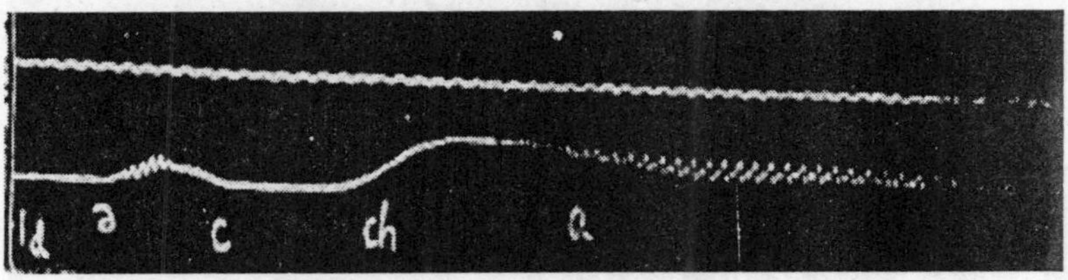

d

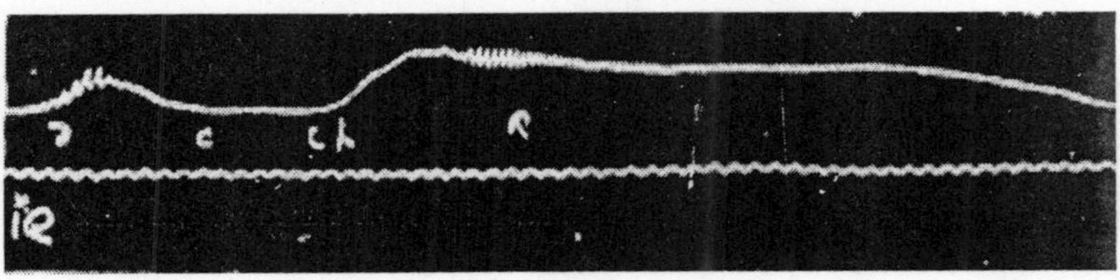

e

Wave Forms

/Jahi/

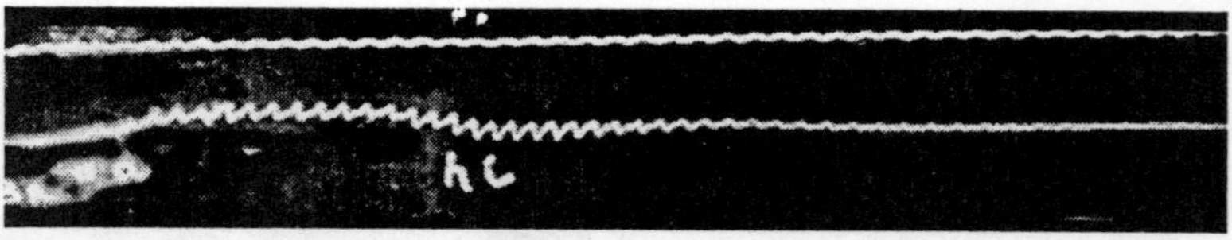

a

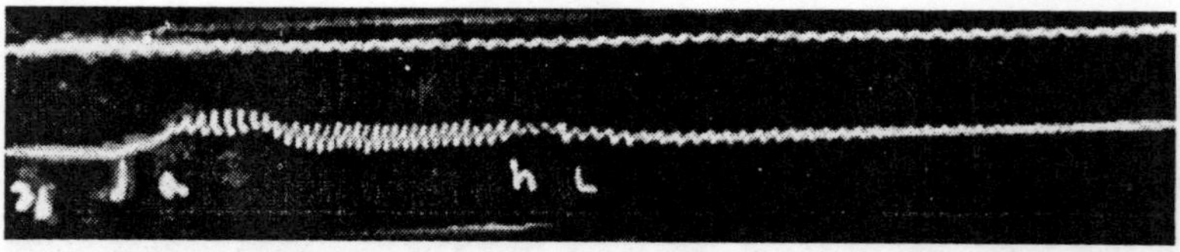

b

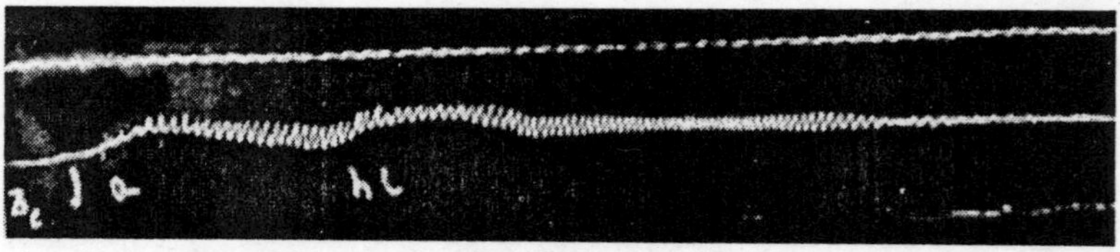

c

/həm roṭi kham/

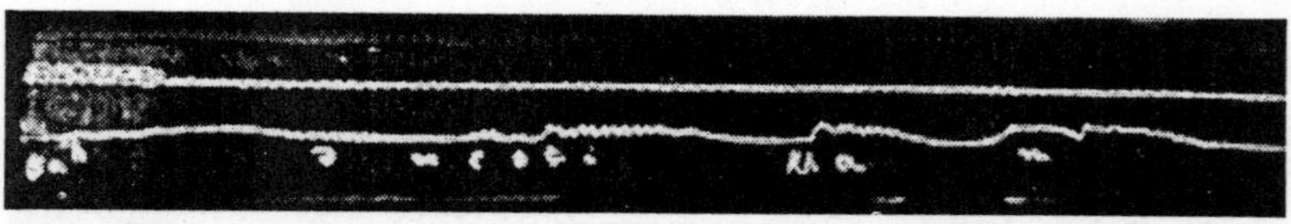

a

b

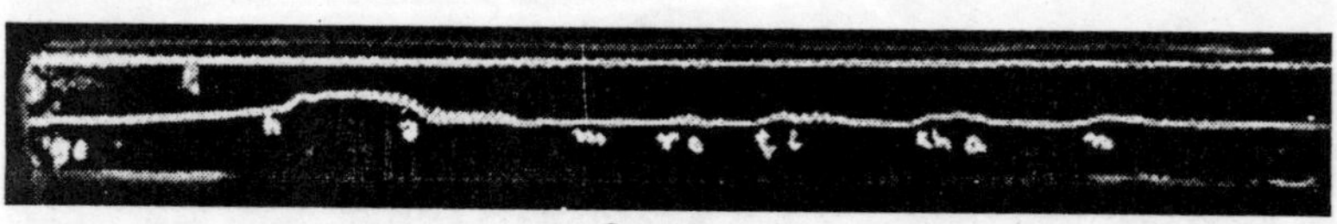

c

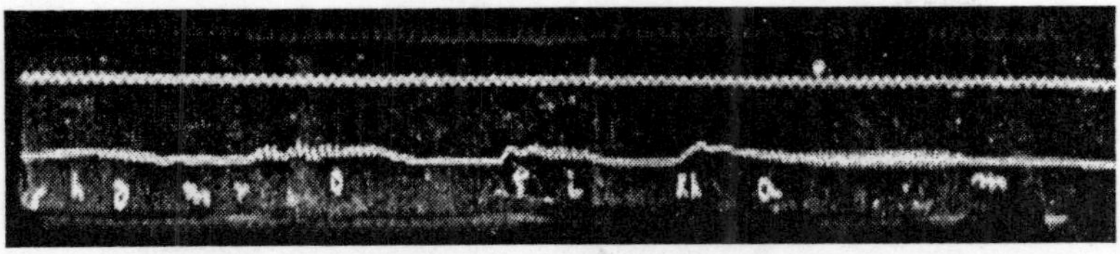

d

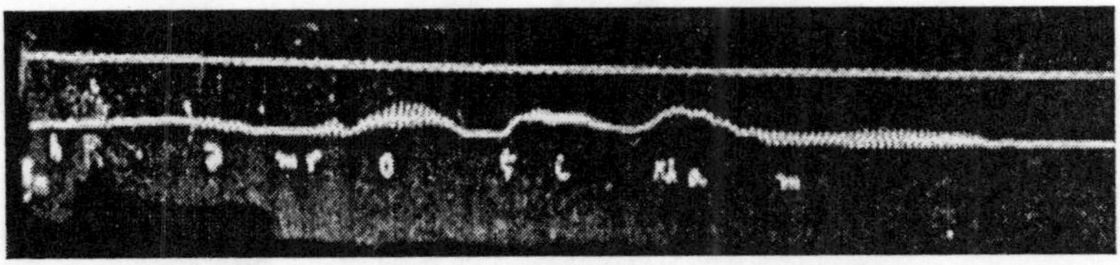

e

/bəṛki nə͜i choṭki/

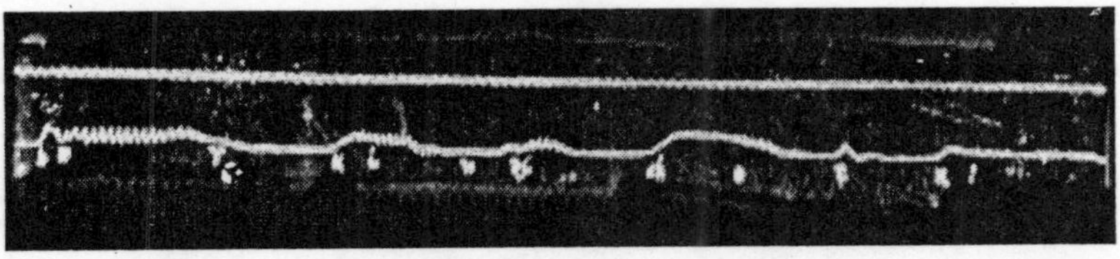

a

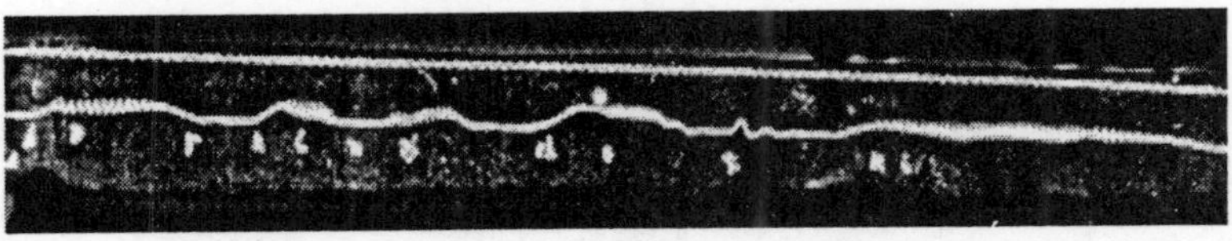

b

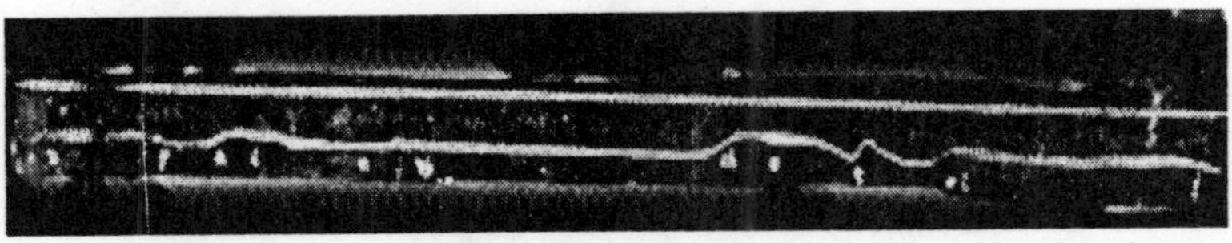

c

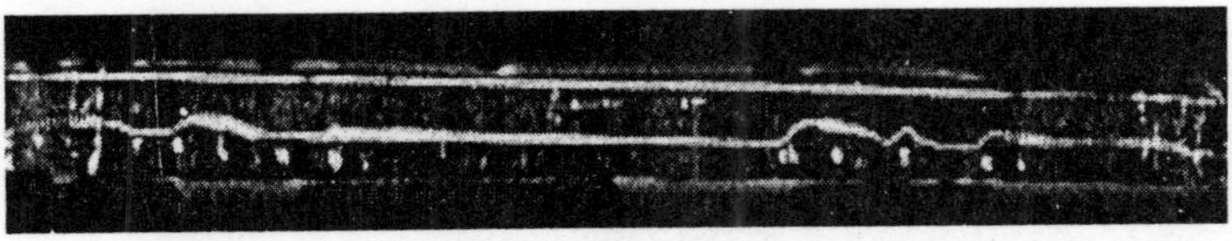

d

Section III

COMPONENTIAL ANALYSIS

9

DISTINCTIVE FEATURES

Introductory

Distinctive features may be regarded as the ultimate components which constitute the phonological system of a language, differentiating morphemes from each other. This principle is assumed on the basis of the binary oppositions which exist either between the presence and absence of a certain quality. In other words, each of the distinctive features involves a choice between two terms of an opposition that displays a specific property, different from the properties of other oppositions.[1] Thus a phoneme may be assumed as a bundle of distinctive features.

These components are built up of their auditory qualities. Inspite of the apparent variety of phonetic characterization of phonemes, this principle can interprete the entire sound system of a language.

The distinctive features of Magahī are analysed here on pure articulatory basis.

Types of Distinctive Features

At first distinctive features are divided into two classes : 1. prosodic and 2. inherent. The prosodic features of Magahī have been described in preceding chapters (6 to 8), (Section II). In Magahī there are twelve distinctive features which are : 1. Vocalic/non-vocalic, 2. Consonantal/non-consonantal, 3. Nasal/oral, 4. Tense/lax, 5. Voiced/voiceless, 6. Discontinuous / continuant, 7. Front/back, 8. High/low, 9. Labial/non-labial, 10. Retroflex/non-retroflex, 11. Dental/non-dental and 12. Front off-glide/back off-glide.

Out of them Front off-glide/back off-glide and High/low are redundant for consonants (except frictionless continuants), on the one hand and Dental/non-dental and Retroflex/non-retroflex are redundant for vowels on the other hand.

These distinctive components will be listed later as a table in plus and minus terms showing their presence and absence respectively.

Some of them are intermediate occuring in between their two polar qualities, symbolised here by ±.

Their description follows :

Vocalic/Non-vocalic

Vocalic phonemes are the results of vibration of vocal cords as the primary sound source together with a free passage through the vocal tract.

The vocal phonemes of Magahī are :

/i I e ə a o U u ə͜i a͜i o͜i u͜i ə͜u a͜u e͜u i͜u m n l r ṛ w y/

Others are non-vocalic.

Consonantal/Non-consonantal

Consonantal phonemes are characterized by an obstruction in the vocal tract.

These are the consonantal phonemes of Magahī : /p t ṭ c k b d ḍ j g ph th ṭh ch kh bh dh ḍh jh gh s h m n l r ṛ w y/

Others are non-consonantal.

These two distinctive features, mentioned above provide four major classes of the phonemes :

(a) Vocalic, non-consonantal : /i I e ə a o U u ə͜i a͜i o͜i u͜i ə͜u a͜u e͜u i͜u/,
(b) Vocalic, consonantal : /m n l r ṛ w y/,
(c) Non-vocalic, consonantal : /p t ṭ c k b d ḍ j g ph th ṭh ch kh bh dh ḍh jh gh s h/,
(d) Non-vocalic, non-consonantal. No phoneme of the language lies in this class.

The four-way classification of phonemes suggests a method of division for general linguistics and it is very near to the Hockett's vowel-consonant-semi vowel classification.[2]

Nasal/Oral

Nasal phonemes are characterized by supplemented nasal resonance. This feature distinguishes the nasals /m n/ from the other liquids /r ṛ/, and the nasal vowels from the oral ones. These are the nasal phonemes of Magahī /mn/. Others are oral.

Nasalization is assumed as a supra-segmental feature of the language (chap. 6)?

Tense/Lax

Tense phonemes are characterized by greater action of the vocal tract as opposed to positions of rest. It is accompanied by tenseness and force.

In the given language these are the tense phonemes /ph th ṭh ch kh bh dh ḍh jh gh i e a o u a͜i o͜i u͜i a͜u e͜u i͜u/

Others are lax.

Voiced/Voiceless

Voiced phonemes are characterized by the periodic vibrations of the vocal cords Vs. lack of such vibrations.

The voiced phonemes of Magahī are /b d ḍ j g bh dh ḍh jh gh m n l r ṛ w y i I e ə a o U u ə͜i a͜i o͜i u͜i ə͜u a͜u e͜u i͜u/

Others are voiceless.

Discontinuous/Continuant

Discontinuous phonemes, *i.e.*, 'interrupted'[3] are characterized either by complete closure of the breath force or by recurrent interruptions during the utterance.

These are the dicontinous phonemes /p t ṭ c k b d ḍ j g ph th ṭh ch kh bh dh ḍh jh gh m n r ṛ/

Continuant phonemes are /s h l w y/ and all vowels.

Front/Back

Such phonemes which are articulated by the front part of tongue, are considered as front Vs. back.

These are the front phonemes of the language : /t ṭ c d ḍ j th ṭh ch dh ḍh jh s n l r ṛ y i I e e͜u i͜u/

Back phonemes are /k g kh gh w a o u U a͜i o͜i u͜i a͜u/

Intermediates are /ə ə͜i ə͜u/

It is redundant for bilabials and glottal spirant.

High/Low

High phonemes are characterized by the height of tongue as opposed to the low position of tongue.

This feature is irrelevant for all the consonants, except /w y/

These are high phonemes, /i I U u u͜i i͜u w y/

These are low phonemes, /a a͜i a͜u/ and these are intermediate phonemes, /e ə o ə͜i o͜i ə͜u e͜u/

Labial/Non-labial

Labials are articulated by the contact of both of lips or by the rounding of lips.

/p b ph bh m w o u U o͜i u͜i ə͜u a͜u e͜u i͜u/ are labials. Others are non-labials.

Retroflex/Non-retroflex

Retroflex consonants are made up of the contact of the front of tongue with retroflexion.

It is redundant in respect to vowels.

Retroflexed consonants are /ṭ ḍ ṭh ḍh ṛ/. Other are non-retroflexed consonants.

Dental/Non-dental

Dental phonemes are characterized by the contact of the front of tongue with teeth.

Like the preceding feature it is also not relevant for vowels.

These are dental consonants /t d th dh s l n/. Others are non-dentals.

Front off-glide/Back off-glide

So far Magahī is concerned this feature is assumed only for diphs. The falling diphs., which tend to be front, called front-off glide and those tend to be back called back-off glide. This feature is redundant for all phonemes except diphs.

These are front-off glides /ə̯i a̯i o̯i u̯i/ and these are back-off glides/ ə̯u a̯u e̯u i̯u/

Advantages of the Analysis

The distinctive feature analysis has two advantages in interpreting the sound system of a given language :

> First, it displays the whole phonological structure of a language in terms of binary oppositions having advantages of complementary distribution at all levels. Thus, it is to provide the most economical method of description of phonology.[4]
> Second, it yields the clue for comparing different languages, that is 'a common typological frame for all phonological analysis'.[5]

The distinctive features analysis of Magahī is shown in the following table.

Table 9 : Distinctive Features of Segmental Phonemes

	p	t	ṭ	c	k	b	d	ḍ	j	g	ph	th	ṭh	ch	kh	bh	dh	ḍh	jh	gh	s	h	m	n	l	r	ṛ	w	y
1. Vocalic :	-	·	-	-	-	-	-	-	-	-	-	-	-	-	-	-	-	-	-	-	-	-	+	+	+	+	+	+	+
2. Cconsonantal :	+	+	+	+	+	+	+	+	+	+	+		+	+	+	+	+	+	+	+	+	+	+	+	+	+	+	+	+
3. Nasal :	-	-	-	-	-	-	-	-	-	-	-	-	-	-	-	-	-	-	-	-	-	-	+	+	-	-	-	-	-
4. Tense :	-	-	-	-	-	-	-	-	-	-	+	+	+	+	+	+	+	+	+	+	-	-	+	-	-	-	-	-	-
5. Voiced :	-	-	-	-	-	+	+	+	+	+	-	-	-	--	-	+	+	+	+	+	-	-	+	+	+	+	+	+	+
6. Discontinuous :	+	+	+	+	+	+	+	+	+	+	+	+	+	+	+	+	+	+	+	+	-	-	+	+	-	+	+	-	-
7. Front :		+	+	+	-		+	+	+	-		+	+	+			-	+	+	+	-	+		+	+	+	+		+
8. High :																									-	-	-	+	+
9. Labial :	+	-	-	--	-	+	-	--	--	--	+	-	-	--	-	+	-	-	--	-	--	-	+	-	--	--	-	+	-
10. Retroflex :	-	-	+	-	--	-	-	+	-	-	--	-	+	-	-	--	-	+	-	-	--	-	--	--	--	-	+	-	-
11. Dental :	-	+	-	--	--	-	+	--	--	---	--	+	--	--	--	-	+	-	-	-	+	-	-	+	+	-	-	-	-

	i	I	e	ə	a	o	U	u	əi	ai	oi	ui	əu	au	eu	iu
1. Vocalic :	+	+	+	+	+	+	+	+	+	++	+	+	+	+	+	+
2. Consonantal :	-	-	-	-	-	-	-	-	-	-	-	-	-	-	-	-
3. Nasal :	-	-	-	-	-	-	-	-	-	-	-	-	-	-	-	-
4. Tense :	+	-	+	-	+	+	-	+	-	+	+	+	-	+	+	+
5. Voiced :	+	+	+	±	+	+	+	+	±	+	+	+	+	+	+	+
6. Discontinuous :	-	-	-	-	-	-	-	-	-	-	-	-	-	-	-	-
7. Front :	+	+	+	±	-	-	-	-	±	-	-	-	±	-	+	+
8. High :	+	+	±	±	-	+	+	+	±	-	±	+	±	-	+	+
9. Labial :	-	-	-	-	-	+	+	+	-	-	+	+	+	+	+	+
10. Retroflex:																
11. Dental :																
12. Front off-glide									+	+	+	+	-	-	-	-

REFERENCES

1. *Fundamentals of Language*, Roman Jakobson—Morris Halles, 1956, p. 4.
2. *Manual of Phonology,* Charles Hockett, p. 75.
3. *Preliminaries to Speech Analysis,* Roman Jakobson, C.G.M. Fant, M. Halle, 1955, p. 21.
4. (a) *Korean Phonemics,* Samuel E. Martin, Reedings in Linguistics, 1957, p. 369.
   (b) *The Phonemes of Bengali*, Charles A. Fergusson, Munier Choudhury, Language, v. 36, 1960, p. 54.
5. *Fundamentals of Language,* R. Jakobson, Marris Halle, 1956, pp. 26-27.

APPENDIX-I

TEXTS WITH ENGLISH TRANSLATIONS

General Remarks

(a) Ten texts are given here which are transcribed phonemically. Out of them the first one/nələnda ke khə̃ṛhər/ has been transcribed with the intonation. In other remaining texts, the intonation phonemes are not mentioned. The intonation patterns of Magahī provide a clue by which we can go through all the texts.

Magahī speech has already been divided into four linguistic types, i.e., narrative, interrogative, exclamatory and hortatory. All narrative and hortatory sentences have/↓/ T.C. but they are quite different in their P.Ls. Each of the narrative sentences has /1 2/ P.Ls., on the ohter hand mostly hortatory sentences have /1 2 3/ P.Ls.

Almost all exclamatory sentences have /↑/ T.C. and / 3 4/ P. Ls.

Interrogative sentences mostly have /↑/ or /↓/ T.Cs. and / 1 2 3 4/ P. Ls. Hortatory and interrogative sentences generally show a similar habit in their P. Ls. but they are not similar in their T. Cs.

(b) All texts are followed by their English translations which are not completely literal but keep in mind the sentence pattern of Magahi.

1 2 1
1. ***Nələnda ke khə̃ṛhər***

1 2 1 2 1
(nələnda ke khə̃ṛhər me du go dekhtahər ke batcit ↓)

11 1 2 1 2
ek ↓ nələnda ke dhərhəra dekh ke həmra to bəṛ robai

1 2 3 1
bərə həl ↓ tor kitmət həu ↓

2 1 2 3 1
dosər ↓ ki kəhəni kimət ↑

11 2 2 2 2 2
ek ↓ nəi bhai tor ki bIcar həu ↓

2 1 2 2 1 1 2 1 2
dosər ↓ o ↓ həmra bhi bhari dUkh au ↓ təjjUb hobə həi↓panc

1 2 1 2
səu ghoṛ səbar səhIt ↓ bəkhətIyar khIjli əiləi ↓ au

2 2 1 2 1
pure des pər kəbja kər lelkəi ↓ gIyan ke i bhənḍar me

1 2 3 2 2 1
ag ləga delkəi ↓ au ↓ dekhəte dekhəte ↓ səb khəṛhər ho

2 1
geləi ↓

11 1 2 1
ek ↓ məgər həmra i bat səməjh me nəi ȧbə həi ↓

21 2 3 1 1 3
ki ↓ məgdhIyn səb okra hIyã tələk ↓ bəṛhe kəise del

2
kəi ↑

2 1 21 2 2 1 2 1
dosər ↓ əre ↓ kUlle ke kUlle ↓ bəudh ho gelən həl↓

2 1 2 1 2
bhIchU səb dUsmən se loha ↓ kəise lete həl ↑

11 4 3 2 2 21 2
ek↓ əisən hole həl ↑ cəndər gUpt aur ↓ cənək ke beṭa

4 2 2 3 1 2
səb ↓ əisən ho gel həl ↑ əppən mano mərjad nəi bəca səkəl ↑

2 1 1 3 1 2 2
dosər ↓ məgər əb əphəsos kəre se ki hot ↓ həni səbh ke↓

2 1 1 2 1 3
əppən Itihās se səbək lebe ke cahi ↓ jekra se ↓ i
2 1 1
gIrəl- pəṛəl gəurəb phInU se khəṛa ho jai ↓ IdhIr to ekra
2 1 2 1 21
phInUse bənabe la ↓ sərəkaro cəukənna ho geləi ha↓
11 3 4 2 3 2
ek ↓ əccha ↑ to i bat həi ↑
2 1 2 1 2 3 1
dosər ↓ tõ ki səməjhəni hən ki ↓ gal pər hāth dhər ke ↓
3 1
bəiṭh jaũ ↑
11 2 1 2 3 1 1 2
ek ↓ nəi bhai ↓ əisən kahe səmə jhbəi ↑ əb to həm
1 1 2 1 1 2
səbh ke ↓ nəya Itihās gəṛhna həi ↓ həmmər əisən je bhi
1 1 2
ḍhəhəl pəṛəl dhərohər həi ↓ okra phInUse ek bar khəṛa
1 1 3 2
kər dena həi ↓ həi kI nə ↑
2 1 2 1
dosər ↓ hã bhai ↓

1. Remains of Nālandā

(A talk between two visitors at the site of Nālandā)

First : I feel dejected after seeing the ruins of Nālandā. What do you think?

Second : Did you ask about the cost?

First : No Sir, What's your opinion?

Second : I see. I also feel very much dejected and wonder that Bakhatiyar Khiljee attacked only with five hundred horse soldiers and captured the whole area. He put on fire the great centre of learning and in a glance everything was destroyed.

First : But I do not understand how the people of Magadha allowed him to reach this place?

Second : All had become Buddhist monks. And how the monks could give a fight with the enemy.

First : Did it happen so! The successors of Chandra Gupta and Chanakya behaved like this! They could not even save their honour?

Second : Now is it of any use to feel sorry about it? We should learn a lesson from our history so that the lost honour may be regained. These days the Government also is taking pretty care to revive it.

First : Well, is it true?

Second : What! Do you think that we would sit idle?

First : No Sir, how can I think of such things? We have to create a new history, Our honour which has already been disrespected should be regained. Is it not so?

Second : Of-course, Sir !

2. Səntokh ke phəl

SUkhəni nam ke ego jənni hələi. okra əise to səbhe sukh hələi baki koi bal-gopal nəi hələi. lekIn sUkhəni səntokh se rəhə hələi. ek din u əppən ṭola-pəṛos ke bəṛhi əu lohar se kəhələk—

ghər pIchuəṛba lohərba ho bhəiya more mItba
ego loha ke pĩjəṛa bəna dehĩ
ghər pIchUəṛba bəṛəhəiya ho bhəiya more mItba
ego kaṭh ke kəṭh pUtlIya bənadehĩ

sUkhəni lohar əu bəṛhi se kəh ke ego pĩjəṛa əu kəṭhəpUtli bənba lelək. u kəṭhəpUtli ke əppən beṭa səməjh ke okkər khub seba bhəu kərə həl.

ek dIn bhəgban okra jãce la bhIkhəmənga bən ke sUkhəni hĩ gel. sUkhəni bəṛi pərem se okra bhikh delək. bhIkhəmənga puch lək ki tõ ki cahã hã? tora koi bal bəcca həu ki nəi? ekra pər sUkhəni kəhlək ki həmmər bəcba əbhi to sUttəl həi. nəi to tora həm dekha detoi həl. i sUn ke bhĩkhəmənga okra məne mən əsis deke cəl gel. sUknəni jəb thoṛi der ke bad əppən bəcca ke Uṭhabe la gel to dekhə he ki u kəṭhəpUtli ke jəgəh pər ego nəu dəs məhInna ke ləṛka sUttəl həkəi. sUkhəni i dekh ke bəṛ əcrəj me pəṛ gel au okkər muh se nIkəl pəṛəl ki əre i ki hol, bhIkhəmənga ke khoje la u bəṛ kosis kərlək baki okkər kəhī̃ pəta nəi mIləl. u to okra hĨyã se bhikh mag ke əlop ho gel həl. se u kəise mIl səkət həl. sUkhəni u bUtru ke bhəgban ke əsIrbad man ke okra pale pose ləgəl.

ehi se kəhəl ja he ki səburi ke məjduri mIlə he.

2. The fruit of content

There was a lady by name Sukhani. Though otherwise happy she had no issue. But Sukhani (had reconciled and) was content. One day he said to her neighbours, a carpenter and a blacksmith :

"O my friendly neighbour! my brother blacksmith! you fashion an iron cage.

"O my friendly neighbour! my brother carpenter! you fashion a wooden puppet."

Saying thus Sukhani got a cage and a wooden puppet from the blacksmith and the carpenter. She accepted the puppet as her son and began to attend upon him.

To test her, one day the God went to Sukhani in the disguise of a beggar. With all love she gave him alms. The begger asked her, "What do you want? Have you any issue or not?" On it Sukhani replied, "my son is now sleeping otherwise I could have shown him to you". Having heard this the beggar gave her blessing in his mind and went away. After some time when Sukhani went to awaken her son, she saw a nine or ten months old child sleeping in the place of the puppet. At this she was surprised and at once spoke, "wonder! What has happened"?. She tried much to find out the begger but could not. The beggar had disappeared just after the begging and thus could not be traced. Sukhani accepted the boy as the blessing of God and bagan to attend upon him.

That's why they say content yields the best fruit.

3. cIṛəi͂ ke bIlap

ego pəhaṛ ke coṭi pər cIṛəi͂ səb ke khõta hələi. okra me ego cIrəi͂ əppən bal bəcca ke sath bəṛ sUkh se rəhə hələi. əppən peṭ ke dhUn me səbhe pəheṛba ke nIcce ego khet me cara cUgge la ja həl. ek dInma ke bat he ki ego cIṛəi͂ əppən bəcba ke əppen khõtabe me choṛ ke cara cUgge la nIkəl gel. bhag ke bat he ki u cIṛəiyã ego bəheli ke jal me phə̃s gel. okkər sathi səb to nIkəl bhagal. i səb dekh ke əur əppən bacba səbh ke iyad kər ke u əppən təgdir ke kose ləgəl hai i ki ho gel. dərəd ke mare u bIlap kəre ləgəl,

Upər pəhaṛ pər khõtba
ṭUn ṭUn me ṭUn
robə hot mor bəcba
ṭUn ṭUn me ṭUn
səb mIl khəillƏi kəunla
ṭUn ṭUn me ṭUn
həm hi pəṛəliəi phəndhəba
ṭUn ṭUn me ṭUn
robə hot mor bəcba
ṭUn ṭUn me ṭUn

cIṛiā ke i bIlap sUn ke u bəheli ke pətthər jəisən kəṭhor chati bhi pəsis gel au u cIṛəi͂ ke choṛ delkəi.

3. Lamentations of a Bird

There were some nests of birds on the peak of a mountion. In one of these a bird had been living much happily with his young ones. To feed themselves the birds used to go to a field, beneath the mountain. Once the birds went away in search of grains, leaving his young ones in the nest. Due to his ill luck the bird was caught in the net of a fowler. His companions flew-away. Thus in distress he was reminded of his young ones and blamed his fate, "alas! what has happened to me?" and due to his deep sorrow he started lamenting :

"On the top of a mountain there was a nest. (/ṭUn ṭUn me ṭun/ is the refrain sound which is repeated here at the last of every line, that is a musical notation.) There my young ones were weeping. Though every bird had got his food, only he alas! fell down in the net. His young ones were weeping.

After hearing the lamentations of the bird the heart of the fowler was moved and he released him from the net.

4. kərni ke lekha

ego raja hələ͜i. okra du go ləṛki hələ͜i. dUnhŨ ləṛki ego gUṛUji hĩ pəṛhe la ja hələ͜i. gUrUji jəb dUnhU ke pəṛhəbə həl thIn to bəṛki ke kəhə həl thIn pəṛh sohagi pəṛh. au chotki se kəhə həl thin pəṛh əbhagi pəṛh. ek dIn rani i bat sUn lelək ə͜ur gUrUji se ekkər mane puch lək. gUrUji bətə͜ilthIn ki choṭki ke təgdir me lIkkhəl hə͜i ki ekkər bIyah mərəl ədmi se hotə͜i. ehI se həm ekra əbhagi kəhə͜i hə͜i. jəb rani i sUn lək to okra bəri dUkh hol ə͜u sõc me pəṛ gel. raja se i batu kəh delək. raja sõc lək ki əisən əbhagi beṭi ke ghər me rəkhe ke nə͜i cahi ehi se əppən nə͜ukər ke agyã delək ki choṭki raj kŨwari ke jəngəl me choṛ a͜u · ə͜isne hol. jəngel me rəjkŨwari ke piyas ləg lə͜i a͜u u ego kŨwa pər gelə͜i. ṭhəṛi ṭhəṛi u dekhəl kə͜i ki ego ghər he jekkər kImaṛi ləgəl hə͜i. rajkŨwari okkər kImaṛi khol ke u ghər me jahe a͜u dekhə he ki ego ədmi mərəl pəṛəl he jekra kulle bədən me kãṭa bhõkəl he. i dekh ke rəjkŨwari ke dəya a gel a͜u okkər kãṭa ke ek-ek kərke nIkale ləgəl. jəb akhIr me ə̃khIya ke kəṭba nIkale la rəh gelə͜i to okra pIyas ləgəl. a͜u pani pIye la kũwã pər gel. təlUk rəjkŨwari ke nə͜ukrniyã u mərəlka ədmIyã ke ə̃khIya ke kə̃tba nIkal delək. jə͜ise hi ə̃khIya ke kə̃tba nIkləl u mərəlka ədmIyã ji gel a͜u okkər pəhIla nəjər nə͜ukrani pər pəṛəl. u səməjh lək ki ehI həmmər dehIya ke kə̃ṭba nIkal lək ha. i guni okra se u pərem kəre ləgəl. jəb rajkŨwari i səb dekh lək to okra bəṛ dUkh bhel ki kə͜un gərəj ləgəl ki u pani piye gel. sə̃͜use dehi ke kãṭa to həm nIkal lũ ə͜ur mehənət ke phəl həmmər dasi le gel. khə͜ir becari səbur kərke rəh gel a͜u rani ke bədle nə͜ukrani bən ke u dUnhũ ke seba kəre ləgəl. rətIya ke sUtte bəkhət u roj i ga ke sUttə həl hãth kəngən bec ke lə͜uṛi kherid lũ, je lə̃͜uṛi həl se rani bhel je rani həl se lə̃͜uṛi bhel. ekdIn raja i doha sUn lelək a͜u nə͜ukrani se okker ərəth pUchlək lekIn nə͜ukrani saph se kUch nə͜i bətə͜ilək. kahe ki okra ḍər ləgəhəl ki raja səc bat jan ke kə̃hi həmranəmar det a͜u nə͜ukrani ke əppən rani bəna let. lekIn raja ke cəin nə mIləl a͜u u dohəba ke ərəth jane ləgi behal ho gel. ek rat raja okkər bhed jane la əppən ə̃gUrIya cir lelak ki okra nind nə͜i abe pa͜i. jəb adhi rat hol to rajkUmari ohI dohəba ga ga ke ro rəhəl həl. i sUnke raja okra pas gel a͜u phInU ekkər ərəth pUch lək. pəhIle to rajkUmari nə͜i bətə͜i lək pər bad me raja ke jId kəre pər səb kUch bəta de lək. raja i sUn ke nəukrani pər bəṛi gossa hol a͜u okra tərhəra khən ke gəṛ delək a͜u rajakUmari se bIyah kər ke sUkh cə͜in se rəhe ləgəl.

4. The fate

There was a king who had two daughters. The girls used to study under a tutor. The tutor while teaching, used to say to the elder one, "read, o fortunate girl, read!" and to the young one "Read o unfortunate girl read" One day the queen heard it and asked him about the reason behind it. The tutor explained that it was written in the fate of the younger daughter that she would be married to a dead body. And for this reason, he called her as 'unfortunate girl'. When the queen knew it she was very much worried. She told it to the king. The king thought that he should not allow such an unfortunate girl to live in the palace and as such ordered his servants to desert her in a jungle. So was it done.

In the jungle the princess felt thirsty and went to a well. While standing by the side of the well she saw a house with its door closed. The princess entered the house after opening its door and found a dead body pierced all over with thorns. Having seen it the princess felt compassion towards it and began to take out the thorns one by one. When only a thorn in the eye was left, she felt thirsty and went to the well for water, Meanwhile her maid servant picked up the thorn from the eye of the dead body. When the thorn from the eye was taken out the dead person was revived. And the first person to be seen by him was the maid servant. He, therefore, thought that she was responsible to take out thorns from his body, and was attracted towards her. When the princess saw, she suffered from deep sorrow : "It was indeed my ill luck that I went for water. I took out every thorn from his body but at last I was deprived of the fruit by my maid servant" she thought. But she faced it with patience and started attending upon them as a maid servant, though a princess. At every night, before sleeping she used to sing a song, "After selling my bracelet, I had purchased a maid servant but alas! the one who was a maid servant became a queen and the one who was a princess became a maid servant."

One night the king heard her singing and asked her as to what its meaning was. But she did not reveal the truth straight way as she was afraid that after knowing it the king might kill her and accept her maid servant as his queen. But the king was restless and very much impatient to know the meaning of the verse. One night (out of anxiety) to know the mystery, the king made a cut in his finger. After mid night he heard the princess weeping and singing her verse. Having heard it the king went to her and again asked the meaning. At first the princess did not tell anything but at his repeated requests she disclosed the matter.

When the king came to know of it, he was full of anger and burried the maid servant in a ditch. There after he married the princess and led a happy life.

5. gIrhəst jibən

ego brahəmən ke du go ləṛki hələ͜i. jəb dUnnU jUwan ho gelə͜i təb ego to əppən bIyah kər lelək ə͜ur dosər sədhUyan bən gel. kUch bərIs ke bad je sədhUyan bən gel həl u sõcələk ki sənyas jibən gIrhəst jibən se bəṛhiyã nə͜i he. gIrhəst jibən me səbhe kUch he. ə͜isən sõc bIcar ke Uho gIrhəst jibən me pərbes kərlək a͜u əppən bIyah kər lelək.

pər kərni ke lekha ke jane he. okkr mərəd koṛhi ho gel. u bəṛi hIkmət se əppən koṛhi mərəd ke səba kərela sUrU kərlək. akhIr bhəgbano okkər pərathəna sUn lel thIn a͜u okkər mərəd kəncən jəisən nIrməl ho gel. dUnhU ke jibən əb bəṛi sUkh se bItte ləgəl ə͜ur dUnnU pərani ke gIrhəsti bəs gel.

akhIr me dUnhU əppən pərIbar səmet sUərəg gel.

5. Family Life

There was a brahmin who had two daughters. When they came of age, one of them got married while other became a nun. After some years the one who was a nun, thought that nonastic life is no better than family life. There is every sort of pleasure in family life. Having decided thus she started taking interest in family life and got married.

The ways of destiny are beyond the reach of knowledge. Her husband became a laper. She started serving her husband, the laper with great care. Her prayer to the God was fruitful and he (her husband) became as pure as gold. And afterwards both of them started a new happy married life.

At last they ascended to heaven along with the members of their families.

6. ənbolti rani

ego rajkŨwar həl jekra əppən rani se kəbhIyo nə͜i pəṭṭə həl. rajkŨwar bəhUt dIne se əppən ghərbali se bədla lebe la sõcə həl. u beṛ korsis kərlək baki okra se kUccho nə͜i bən səkəl. okkər rənia bəṛi cəlãk həl. rajkŨwar jəb əppən rani se bədla nə͜i le səkəl to u gossa ke mare ghəre se nIkəl gel. u ego ə͜isən raj me cəlte cəlta pəhŨcəl jəhã ke rajkŨwari nə͜i bolə həl. rajkŨwar u ənbolti rajkŨwari ke pas gel a͜u okra bolabe la bəṛ-bəṛ hIkmət kəre Iəgəl. kUcche dIn me rajkŨwar u ənbolti rani ke pərem jal me phə̃s gel.

Iddhir okkər rani bhi okra khojte khojte okkər piche cələlo u ənbolti rajkŨwari ke i pərtIgyã hələ͜i ki je okra bole la məjbur kər det u okra se əppən bIyah kər let. rəjkŨwar ke ghərbali ke jəb i bat malUm bhel to u bəṛI phIkkIr me pəṛ gel a͜u sõce ləgəl ki ə͜isən kə͜un Upa͜i kərŨ jekra se okkər raja ke mən ke mUrad pura ho ja͜i. bəṛi sõc bIcar ke u ego ə͜isən tərkib nIkal lək jekra se u ənbolti rani jərur ke bol det. u əppən raja ke cUppe cUppe mədət kəre ləgəl au ekdIn əisən hol kI akhIr me ənbolti rani ke okkər celãki se bole pəṛəl. ekra pər ənbolti rani ke bIyah u raja ke sath ho gel.

i səb bat jəb u raja ke malUm hol to okkər əcrəj ke ṭhIkana nəi rəhəl. u əppən ghər bali se har manlelək au dUnhũ rənIyn ke sath hIlmIl ke rəhe ləgəl.

6. Reticent Princess

Once there was a king who was not on good terms with his queen. For many days he thought of taking a revenge of his wife. He tried much but could not do anything. The queen was very clever. When the king could not take revenge, he left the palace in anger.

After travelling a lot he reachd a kingdom, the princess wherein had kept dumb. The king went to the reticent princess and tried much to make her speak. He afterwards fell in love with the reticent princess.

On the other hand his queen also followed him to find out the king. The reticent princess had taken an oath that she will marry only the person who will compell her to speak. Coming to know of this, the queen was grieved and started thinking how she could be helpful to her king in fulfilling his desire. After thinking a lot she got a method by which the reticent princess could surely be made to speak. Without the knowledge of the king she began to help him. At last, one day, owing to her cleverness the reticent princess had to speak. Afterwards the king married the reticent princess.

When the king came to know of all what had happened, he was surprised. He accepted defeat from his wife and led a happy life with both of his queens.

7. sami raj raje raj

ego raja hələi jekra satgo beṭi hələi. jəb səb pəṛh lIkh ke hosIyar ho geləi to ek dIn raja sato beṭike bolake puchələk ki tũ səb kekkər raj pəsənd kərə hĩ. ekra pər chəbo beṭi kəhəl kəi ki həmra la bape raj səbse bəṛhIyā̃ həi. lekIn okra me choṭki beṭi kUch nəi bol ləi. to raja phInU okra se ehI bat pUchəl kəi. ekra pər choṭki beṭi jəbab deləl ki sami raj raje raj. i jəbab sUn ke raja bəṛi gossa ho gel aur əppən məntri ke agyā del kəi ki choṭki rajkUmari la ego əisən bər khojəl jai jekra nə to khai ke rəhe nə pie ke au ghər-dUwar bhi nəi ho. məntri əisən bər khoj te khojte thək geləi baki koi nəi mIləl. akhIr me okra ego bhIkhəməŋga mIləl jekra pəkəṛ ke u raja ke samne le geləi. raja okra dekh ke bəṛ khUs hol au Uhi bhIkhəməŋgba ke hā̃th əppən chotki rajkUmari ke hā̃th de dələk. u bhIkhəməŋgba i səb dekh ke bəṛi əkcəkəiləi ki kəhā̃ həm bhIkhəməŋga au kəhā̃ i rajkUmari. ehi sõc ke u bhIkhəməŋga rajkUmari ke əppen sath le jai la nəi təiyar ho ləi. pər raja ke ḍərabe dhəmkabe se u məjbur ho gel. becara bhIkhəməŋga age age cələl əu rəjkUmari okkər piche piche. rəsta me ego nəddi mIl ləi. jəb dUnhU pərani nədIya par kər rəhəl həl to u BhIkhəməŋgba ego lal dekhəl kəi au okra sədhrən cij janke pani se nIkal lelək. jəb nəddi ke par al to dekhələk ki ojja bəhUt sa ləṛəkən gẽd khel rəhəl ha. i dekh ke u bhi əppən lal ke nIkal ke okra sath khele ləgəl. i cij ke ego ədəmi dekh lelək ki i bhIkhəməŋga lal se khel rəhəl ha au jake u ibat hŨyā̃ ke raja se kəh delək. raja əppən nəuker ke bhej ke u bhIkhəməŋga ke bola bhejlək. rəjkUmari thək ke hŨe pər ego jhopṛi me sUt geləi həl. raja okra se lal le leləkəi au okra khub əccha bhojən khai la deləkəi. əbhIyo tək bhIkhə məŋga ke kUch pəta nəi he ki okra etna adər khatIr kahe la kərəl ja rəhləi ha. sehi se u adha khəikəi au adha rajkUmari ləgi le jai ləgələi. to raja kəhəl kəi ki tũ bhər peṭ kha le həm rajkUmari ləgi tUrte ek thal bhojen bhej de hləi. u raja rajkUmari la ek thal bhojən au sat gaṛi rUpəiya pəisa jəbahIrat se bhər ke u jhopəṛiya me bhej del kəi jekra me rajkUmari əbtək sUttəl həl. rajkUmari jəb jəgləi to okra i səb kUcch nəi səməjh pəṛəlai lekIn jəb u raja ke cIṭhIya pəṛhəl kəi to səbhe bat səməjh me əiləi. əb rajkUmari ohi dhən se ego bəṛi bhari məhəl bənba lelək au u bhIkhəməŋga əb raja gUrba ke nam se məshur ho geləi. i tərəh rajkUmari raja gUrba ke sath sUkh cəin. se rəhe ləgəl au sami raj raje raj ke bat səc ho gel.

7. The Kingdom of Husband

There was a king who had seven daughters. When all of them had finished their studies and grown wise, one day the king called them and asked each one of them as to whose kingdom would every one of them like? On this six of them replied that they would like their father's kingdom which is the best one for them. But among them the youngest daughter did not speak anything. So, the king again asked her the same question. Then the youngest daughter answered that her husband's kingdom would be the best one for her. Hearing thus the king became very angry and ordered his minister to find a bridegroom for his youngest daughter who had neither food for eating, nor house to live in. His minister tried his best but did not find such a bridegroom. At last he came accross a beggar. He presented him before king. After getting him the king became very happy and to that beggar he married his youngest daughter.

In these circumstances the beggar was wondering all the time. "It is all funny. How a princess and a beggar can go together" he thought. The beggar, therefore, was not ready to go along with the princess. But at the last moment he was forced to accept her.

The poor fellow started his journey. He was followed by his wife, the princess. On their way they had to cross a river. While they were crossing the river the beggar saw a precious stone in the water and took it out as an ordinary stone. When they had crossed the river he saw many boys playing with a ball on the bank of the river. Having seen it he also took out the stone and started to play with it. Some one noticed that a beggar was playing with a precious stone and told the king of the beggar's whereabouts. The king ordered his men to fetch the beggar. The princess, who was completely tired by that time slept in a cottage nearby. The king took the precious stone from the beggar and gave him a very delicious meal. Still the beggar could not make out the reason why the king entertained him. The beggar, therefore, ate half of the meal and left of it for his wife. Seeing this the king told him, "you eat as much as you like. I will send a very good dish for your wife."

The king sent a delicious dish and seven carts full of coins and diamonds. When the princess got up she did not first make out anything but from the letter of the king she understood every thing. Now the princess built a grand palace with the money and the beggar became known as "Raja Gurba". In this way the princess started her glorious happy life with Raja Gurba and the phrase "the Kingdom of the husband is the best one" came true.

8. mUrda se bIyah

ego rəjkŨwari ke təkdir me lIkkhəl həl kI okkər bIyah barəh bərIs ke mUrola se hot. kUch dIn ke bad səcce me ə͜isən ho gel. ekra pər bəṛi hIkmət kərəl gel a͜u rəjkŨwari ke bhag se u murda ji Uṭhəl. baki ji ja͜i pər u mUrda je ego raja həl dhokha se u rəjkŨwari ke dəsIe se okra rəjkŨwari səməjh ke sadi kər keløk. pər thoṛIke dInma ke bad bhənḍa phUṭ gel. i jan ke U raja je pəhIle mUrda həl bəṛi dUkhi bhel. akhIr me raja əppən bIyahi ə͜urət ke pəhəcan lək a͜u u rejkŨwari ke əpna lelək. təb səb mIlke sUkh se rəhe ləglən.

8. Marriage with a Dead Body

It was written in the fate of a princess that her marriage would be settled with the dead body of a person who had died before twelve years. And later the prophesy came true. Because of the good luck of the princess, with great difficulty the dead body was revived. After being revived the (dead) person—previously a prince—married a maid servant of the princess. The prince could know the truth only after some days. After coming to know what was the truth, the revived prince was very much grieved. At long lost he could recognise his wife and afterwards led a happy life with her.

9. cənnən ke koila

ego jəngəl me ego məllah rəhə hələi. u bəṛi gərib dUkhIya hələi. əppən din dUnIyā̃ cəlabe la u roj jəngəl ke ləkṛi kaṭ ke jəlabə həl au okkər koila səhər jake bec de həl. IhI okkər roj dInma ke kam rəhə həl. i tərəh se u jəngəl roj kəṭ te kəṭ te ekdIn saph ho gələi. i dekh ke məllah ke bəṛi phIkIr ho geləi kI əb okkər roji rojgar kəise cələt. əb u ki kərət·ehI phIkIr me əbrI u ləkəṛIya ke nəi jəleilək au sUkhəle okra bece ləgi səhər le gel. əbki bar bəjriya me okkərələkəṛike bəṛ mol hol au u bəri bhari dam me bIkkəl. bat i hələi ki u ləkṛi cənnən ke həl ohĩ bəjəh se okkər etna dam bhel.

i dekh ke məllah becara əppən matha ṭhok lelək. IhI bat okra pəhIle se malUm hot həl to əb tək u ketna malomal ho jat həl. pər əb ki kərū̃. əb to jəngəlIo kəṭ ke məsan bən gel ha· okkər təgdir ketna khərab həi ·pər əb pəchətabe hot ki jəb cIṛIyā̃ cUg gel khet.

ehI se kəhəl jahe ki ədmi ke hər kam khub ṭhok bəja ke au səməjh bujh ke kəre la cahi.

9. Coal of Sandalwood

There was a fisherman living in a jungle. He was very poor. Daily he cut the wood of the jungle and burnt it. He sold the coal in market for his livelihood. That was his every day routine. Thus diminishing every day the whole jungle was virtually destroyed. The fisherman, therefore, became very serious and thought as to how his livelihood would continue and what will he do now? In this disturbed state of mind he did not charred the wood and carried it to sell in the market. This time the wood fetched a very high price in the market. The reason why it fetched a high price was that it was sandalwood.

Bocoming aware of what he had done, the fisherman, in distress struck his forehead with his hand. If he had known it before hand he could have become rich, thought he. But now it was of no use. He had cut the whole jungle and put to ashes.

How unlucky he was ! But now it was not of any avail as it was no more.

And therefore they say that one should act thoughtfully.

10. sona ke kes bali rəjkŨwari

ego raja ke du go ləṛki həlai. bəṛki ke nam dhənmaiti au choṭki ke nam bəlmaiti həlai. choṭki bəṛi khubsurət həlai au okkər sona ke kes həlai.

ek dIn donnu bəhInIyã nəddi me nəhai gelai. nəhaite nəhaite choṭki bəhInIyã ke ego kesIya Ukhəṛ gelai. ekra pər u sõc lək ki i kesIa kəhã phekũ. u ghəṛi nədIya ke dhərba me ego bel bəhəl cələl a rəhəl həl· okra u le lelək au okra əppən ṭUṭəlka kesIya se ləpeṭ ke bəha delək. ego rəjkŨwar ke nəjər okra pər pəṛəl. rəjkũwar ke dost u belba ke nIkal ke la delək. rəjkŨwar dekhəl kai ki okra pər sona ke kes ləpeṭəl hai. i dekh ke okkər ãkh cõdhIya gelai au u məne məne sõce ləgəl ki i kesIya jəb etna sUnnər he to ekkər malkIn kaisən hot. həm to okra khojəm au okre se bIyah kərəm. au kesIya ke u əppən dhotIya me bãdh lelək. i bat sõcte sõcte u əppən ghər a gel.

okra se nəto khal gel au nə pIəl. u bhəla kəise kthat həl. okra to jUṛba dhər lelək həl. nə to kekro sath u hõsai au nə bolai.hər səmai kesiya ke əppəu chətiya seləgaile rəhai. okkər i desa dəkh ke raja-rani kəhe ləgəl dekha dekha rəjkũwar ke ki ho gelo ha. koi gUni gani baid ke bolaba. raj bhər ke bəṛ bəṛ baid al. baki okkər rog ke pəta kekro nə ləgəl.

raj məhəl me ego kUṭni bUṛhIya həlai. U kəhlək ki həmra ego cərkha au thoṛa rua da. həm bətlaibau ki rəjkŨwar ke ki ho gelo ha. bUṛhIya ke ego cərkha au ruiya del gel. bUṛhIya okra leke rəjkŨwar ke nəjdik pəhŨcəl au cərkha cəlabe ləgəl. cərkha se roĩ roĩ ke əbaj nIklə həl. rəjkŨwar i sUn sUn ke kUṛh gel au boləl dUr ho, dur ho, hIyā cərkha kaṭe la kahe la baiṭhəna hã. bUṛhIya pUchəl kai əre beṭa tora kaun bImari ho gelo ha. ekra pər rəjkŨwar bol lai kəhe se ki hot. tũ ki pura kər dema. bUṛhIya bol lai hã raja tũ jaisən kəhəma oisən kərbau. təb rəjkŨwar kəhəl kai ki i kes ke dekh. u kes ke dekh ke bUṛhIya hõse ləglai au bol ləi ekre la tũ mUh kan phUləule hə̃la. dur ho. Uṭh jo beṭa au kho pi. həmtor bImari səməjh gelləu okkər Upai həm kərə həkIəu.

u bUṛhIya rəjkŨwar ke təsbir le ke u rəjkŨwari ke khoje la cələl. rəsta me cəlte cəlte kəik dIn ho gel. akhIr me okra pəta cələl ki ehI raj me u rejkŨwari rəhə he jekker kes sona əisən sUnnər he. bUṛhIya dekhəhe ki u dUnhu bəhIn nəddi me nəhai la ja rəhəl ha. bUṛhIya rajkŨwari ke jãcela cah lək ki jəra dekhũ ki jəisən rəjkŨwari ke kes he oisne okkər dIlbo he ki nəi. au bəhana bəna ke rəsta me loṭ loṭ ke bIlap kəre ləgəl hai re dəiya hai re dəiya əb nə bəcbəu mər jəi bəu. okkər robai sUnke səbbhe ṭhIṭhək gel. bəṛki rəjkŨwari kəhələk u rə̃ṛIya kahe la ro rəhəle ha. phaltu phaltu ke nəkkəl mar rəhəle ha. ekra pər choṭki rəjkũwari boləlkəi u becari to bIpət ke marəl həi. həm to okkər bIpət sUn lem. I kəhə ke u bUṛhIya ke pas gel au okra se batcit kəre ləgəl. bUṛhIya okkər həthəba me rəjkŨwar ke təsbIrĩya delək au bol lək i rjkŨwar tora la pəran bisar rəhəlo ha okker tũ jan bəca le.

kŨwari bəlməiti jəb u təsbir ke dekhələk to okkər dhirəj dol gel. əppen ə̃cra me u təsbir ke nUka lelək au məhəl ləuṭ gel. khəṭbas pəṭbas le lelək. ən pani tIyag delək. səkhi səb se hə̃se bole a choṛ delək. raja rani əppən beṭi ke i halət dekh ke səb bat səməjh lelək. rəjkŨwar ke təsbir dekh ke apIs me kəhe ləglən ki əb həmmər beṭi la bər mIl gel. raja əppən məntri ke bhej ke bIyah ke dIn ṭhik kəra lelək. i səb dekh ke əṛki bəhInIya sõce ləgəl ki etna əccha rəjkŨwar se okkər bIyah ho rəhəl ha au həm əisĩ ke əisĩ rəh jam. u nIhəcəi kəilək ki bIyah ke dInma bəlməiti ke beni ke səng nag nagIn ke gũth dem to u mər jat au bad me u rəjkŨwar se həmmər sadi ho jat.

u səcce me əisne kərlək. bIyah ke pəhIle okkər beni me nag-nagIn ke gũth delək. nag nagIn okra kaṭe ləgəl au u bIkh se bIyakUI hoke sUt gel. jəb okkər mai uṭhabe ləgəl to bəlməiti boləl :

kəise UṭhIəu kəise ake bəiṭhIəu
bəṛki didi gũth delthIn nagnagIn beni
Upre se khə̃s delthIn korIək phul
akhIr me bəlməiti mər geləu. i

səb jan ke rəjkŨwar də͜uṛəl al a͜u kahə lək ki həm əppən rani ke cənnən ke cIta pər jəlabəm. okkər rakh lete jam.

rejkũwar okkər rakh ke sona ke ḍIbba me sənjo ke rəkh lək. ekdIn rəjkŨwar kəhĩ cəl gel to u ḍIbba se ego sUnnər rajkŨwari nIkəl ke kəmra ke səb cij sərIya ke phInU okra me ghŨs gel. rəjkŨwar koṭhəri me jəb al to koṭhərIya məh məh məhək rəhəl həl. rəjkŨwar ekkər karən jane la korsis kəre ləgəl. okkər koṭhəri me ke abə he i pəta ləgabela u chIp gel. u rəjkŨwari phInu nIkəs ke səb kUch saph kəre ləgəl. rəjkŨwar i dekh ke təjjUb me pəṛgel. u rəjkŨwari ke ja ke pəkəṛ lelək a͜u kəhe ləgəl əb həmra choṛ ke tũ kəhĩ mət jo. nə͜i to həmme bhi mər jə͜i bə͜u. həm to əb tora nə͜i choṛ bə͜u.

ekra pər u dUnhũ pərani apəs me mIl gel a͜u dUnhU sUkh se rəhe ləgəl.

10. The Princess of Golden Hair

There was a king who had two daughters by name Dhanmaiti and Balmaiti. Balmaiti who was younger was very beautiful and had golden hair.

Once both sisters went to a river to take bath. While bathing a hair of the younger sister fell down. She did not know where to throw it. Meanwhile a round fruit was flowing in the current of the river. She took it and put her hair around it and threw it in the river. The fruit caught the attention of a prince. A friend of the prince picked it up from the river. The prince saw the golden hair tied on it. With his eyes spread at its sight, he thought : "if the hair is so beautiful how beautiful must the woman be of who it is? I will find out and marry her." He kept it in his lower garment and reached his house thinking about her.

He could not eat or drink. How could be he eat? He was suffering from love fever. He could not laugh or talk. He always put the hair at his heart. After noticing his condition the king and queen said to each other look, how the prince is suffering? Call some experienced physician". Many great physicians of his kingdom came but no one could diognize the disease.

There was an old woman who was very clever. She told the king, "Give me a charkha and some cotton. I will tell you what is the reason of his suffering". A charkha and some cotton was given to the old woman. Afterwards the old woman went to the prince and began to move her charkha which put forth an irritating noise. At this the prince was very angry and said, "Go away, go away from me. What is the use to move a charkha here?"

The old woman asked him, "O son! What are you suffering from?"

The prince replied, "What is the use of teeling it to you? Would you help me?"

She answered, "Yes, my prince. I will do if you wish so".

The prince said to her, "Look at the hair".

The old woman began to laugh after seeing it and said to him, "Only for this reason you became so sad! O my dear! you get up and start your usual routine. I came to know your disease and I will try my best".

The old woman took a picture of the prince and started on a journey to find out the princess. She travelled for many days. At last she reached the kingdom where the princess with golden hair lived. The old woman observed that both the sisters were daily coming to a river for taking bath. She wanted to know the nature of the princess, "Let me see, how is her heart? Is there any similarity between her heart and her beautiful hair?" She thought. She fell down on the way and began to cry, "alas! I may not servive, I am dying". None paid, any attention to her cries. The elder princess said "why the widow is weeping? Why she is creating a scene?" On the other hand the younger princess said, "I would listen to the poor woman and know what is her trouble". After that she went to the old woman and had talked to her. The old woman handed over the picture to the princess and said, "This prince is dying for you. Please save him".

At the sight of the picture the princess was surprised and was attracted towards it. She hide the picture in her sari and returned to the palace. She was confined to bed and indifferent toward meals. She did not participate in the jokes of her friends. The king and the queen understood every thing after seeing the condition of their daughter. They saw the picture of the prince and said, "now we have got the bridegroom for our daughter". With the help of his minister the king fixed the date of their marriage. The elder sister became jealous that her marriage was to be held with such a beautiful prince and that herself should remain unmarried. She planned to tie a male and female cobra in her braid on the day of marriage, as a result which she (i.e. younger sister) would die and herself would be married to the prince.

And she did accordingly. Before marriage she arranged her sister's braid with a male and a femal cobra. The cobras beat the younger sister as a result of which she fell unconcious. When her mother went to wake her up, Balmaiti said, "mother! how can I get ready and how can I sit there? My elder sister has tied in my braid a male and a female cobra and to conceal them she fixed kari flawer on them.

At last Balmaiti died. The prince, when he came to know all this, hurried to the queen and said that he will burn his wife on the pyre of sandalwood and will take her ashes.

The prince preserved her ashes in a golden box. One day when the prince had been out somewhere, a beautiful princess came out from the box and arranged the bed room and again entered into the box. When the prince came back he noticed an unusual smell. The prince wanted to know the reason behind it. To catch the unnoticed visitor he hid himself in the room. The princess again came out and began to arrange the room. The prince wonder-struck caught hold of the princess and said to her, "you do not leave me otherwise I will also die. Now I will not leave you".

Afterwards they were united and led a happy married life.

Appendix–II

MAGAHI LEXICON

ə

ə̃khIya	eye
ə̃g	organ
ə̃gUrIya	finger
ə̃car	pickle
ə̃cra	a part of sari
ə̃dhera	darkness
ə̃ṛ	to stick
ə̃ṛəl	stuck
ə̃sna	a month of winter (Ashwin)
əkəlmənd	wise
əkar	size
əkkhəṛ	obstinate
əkcəkə̃ilə̃i	surprised
əkṛa	rough rice
əkhəroṭ	a dry fruit
əg	world
əgəst	an English month (August)
əgaṛi	forward
əgIn	fire
əgor	wait
əghən	a month of winter (Agrahayana)
əgha	to satisfy
əntIm	last
əntra	an element of music
əndhar	drakness
ənṭi	a bundle of thread
ənṭsənṭ	worthless
ənbolti	silent, (f) dumb
əpna	to accept, own
əppen	own
əpsuiya	unmarried girl
əphəsos	repetant
əb	now
əbaj	şound
əber	clear weather
əber	clear weather
əbera	clear weather
əbki	this chance, again
əbrI	this chance, again
əbtek	till now
əbhaga	unfortunati (m.)
əbhagi	unfortunate (f.)
əbhi	now
əbhi	just now
əbhIyo	even now
ə̃gho	to satify

əghai	to be satisfied
əghor	dirty
əghori	dirty man
əcərəj	wonder
əcar	pickle
əccha	good, well, o.k.
əcchət	sacred rice
əchar	heavy rain
əjəgUt	wonderful
eji	a sort of address
əjur	request
ədəra	a fortnight of rainy season
ədmi	man
ədmIỹa	man
ədna	ordinary
ədhIye	smallest coin
əmdi	man
əmdur	a guava
əmba	mango
ən	grain
ənar	pomegranate
əndesa	hope, dout
ənker	of another
əngna	court yard
ənt	end
ərəth	meaning
əre	a sort of address
ərui	a sort of vegetable
ərbInd	a name of a boy
ələg	separate
əlUwa	potato
əlop	disappeared
əlblal	off minded
əlgəl	protuberance
əsIrbad	blessing
əsis	blessing
əsthan	place
əsmənnia	sky
əhəsan	obligation
əhir	a caste
əhor	exchange
əhoṭh	uncivilized
əbhīya	just now
əmari	dry pieces of cow-dung

A

ãkh	əye
ãc	fire
ãṭ	a bundle of hay
ãti	a bundle of hay
ãṭh	fruit's stone
ãṭhi	fruit's stone
ãdhi	storm
ãṛ	testicle
a	come
a ke	being come
akhIr	end
ag	fire
age	forward
agỹa	order
aj	to-day
aja	come on
a ja	come and go
ajo	come
aṭh	eight
atUr	impatient

ad	memory
adər	prestige, honour
adha	half
adhi	half
an	next day or dignity
apəs	among
apIs	among
ab	faith
abə	please come
abəl	being come
abahũ	I am coming
abahu	would you come?
am	mango
ari	saw
are	far
al	came
ala	being come
as	hope
ah	cold breath
ahu	please come

I

ĨjorIya	moonlight
Ĩrot	side
Iad	memory
Ikəṭṭhe	in all
IjUn	here
ItIhãs	history
Itna	a sort of quantity
Idhər	here
IdhIr	here, this side
Inar	well
Inkər	his
Inkar	deny
Inc	inch
Injor	light
Iṛot	side
Iyar	friend, lover
Iljam	charge
IhI	this
Ihora	request

i

ĩṭ	brick
i	this
iad	memory
i tərəh	like this
id	a festival of Mohammedans
i bat	this matter
ise	for this reason

U

Ũsau	a process of boiling
Ũh	asort of sound
UkṛU	difficulty
Ukhəṛ	root out
Ug	rise
Uge	rise
Ughən	rop
Ughar	open, put off
UjUr	objection
UcIt	right
Uce	high
Uṭhə	please get up
Uṭhəl	stood, got up
Uṭha	please get up

Uṭhabe	when lifted
Uṭhi	please get up
Uṭhəu	may he get up?
Uṭhjo	get up
Utsah	encouragement
UtahUl	hurry
Udkəl	fastly
Unar	open
Unda	good
Unkha	his
Ungli	finger
Unka	his
Upər	at, on
Upa͜i	method
Upadhi	degree
Upchəl	empty
Upjəl	grown
Upma	simile
Uphəna	to be disappeared
Upa͜i	device
Uphəna	to boil
Ubbe	to be off
Uber	clear weather
Umər	age
Umsəl	much heated
Umṛəl	flooded
Uṛ	fly
Uṛənt	flying
Uṛahəl	cleared
Uljhəl	complexed
Ulṭəl	made up side down
UllU	owl
Uhi	that
Uho	he

u

ũṭ	camel
u	he, that
ub	vexation
un	wool

e

ẽṛ	heel
e	a sort of address
ek	one
ekra	that, him
ekkər	its, his
ekə͜isa	twenty one
ego	one
ejjã	here
etəna	so much
enhĩ	here
ehI	the same
ehIse	for this reason

o

õṭ	side, vote
õs	dew
o	a sort of address
okkər	him, her
okra	him, her
ojja	there
ojha	a superstitious man
oṭ	vote
onhĩ	there
or	the last point
ol	tuber

os	dew
ohari	the forepart of a roof through which water falls
ohI	the same

əi

əio	shall I come?
əiəi	would I come?
əiəu	would I come?
əinə	have you come?
əib	demerits
əibo	would I come?
əima	would you come?
əilə̃	have you come?
əila	have you come?
əiləi	came
əis	luxury
əisən	like this, such
əisne	such, as
əisi	useless
əiseto	usually

ai

ai	a sort of exclamation

oi

oi	a word used while indicating acceptance
oina	name of a village
oisən	like that
oisne	like that

əu

əũkha	a superstitious performance for child
ə̃ura	myrobalan
əu	and
əughər	obstinate
əur	and
əurət	woman
əura	myrobalan

au

au	come, and
aur	and

k

kək həra	the alphabet
kəkh	painfull sound
kəkhəra	a village
kəccha	Underwear
kəjerhəṭIya	a tribe
kəṭ	a sort of sound
kəṭəte	through the procedure of cutting
kəṭar	dagger
kə̃ṭba	thorn
kəṭh	wooden
kəṭhor	hard
kəṭhpUtəlIya	wooden puppet
kətar	line
kəth	catechu

kədoṛa	muddy water
kəngal	beggar, poor
kəngən	bracelet
kəncən	gold
kənghi	comb
kənṭop	a sort of cap
kənṭhi	a sort of religious thread
kənṭh	throat
kəndha	shoulder
kənma	ear, a small weight
kənhai	a popular name
kəpṛa	cloth
kə̃psəl	wept
kə̃pcəl	have cut
kəpcna	hair cutting
kəpṭi	earthen cup
kəpar	head
kəpur	camphor
kəph	bad saliva
kəpphən	shroud
kəbja	occupy
kəbəḍḍi	a ply
kəbhIyo	when
kəmər	waist
kəmra	drawing room
kəmIya	labourer
kər	do
kəre	do
kərə ke	after doing
kərəl	being done
kərə	please do
kəra	please do
kər-lək	did
kərəm	I will do, fate
kərbəu	I will do
kərŨ	shall I do?
kərUwa	bitter
kera	banana
kərja	loan
kər+ja	do some thing
kərəni	fate
kərhĨ	do
kərŨ	shall I do?
kərgha	a sort of wheel
kəl	tomorrow
kəlol	a play with water
kəlsi	water pot
kəlchUl	a kitchen article
kəh	tell
kəhə	please tell
kəhəma	to speak, where
kəhəl	being told
kəhəlkəi	spoke
kəhã	where
kəhĩ	any where
kəhU	please tell
kəhe	tell
kəhlək	told
kəhke	being told
kəhẽr	groan
kəhŨ	would I tell?
kəhni	proverb
kəhəi	let him tell
kajəl	collyrium
kach	an insect of water
kaṭ	cut
kaṭe	to beat

kaṭh	wood
kan	ear
kanpUr	a famous city
kanh	the name of Lord Krishna
kabu	strength
kam	work
kayl	influenced
kar	black
kara	black coloured man
kari	black coloured man
kari	black coloured female
karən	cause, reason
kal	death, time
kahe	why
kahela	for what reason
kIrcI	a bundle of thread
kImaṛi	door
ki	what or that
kin	purchase
kimət	cost
ki+mət	what (is your) opinion
kimti	costly
kUkUr	dog
kUcch	some
kUcho	some thing
kUṭ	a sort of sound for cutting
kUṛh	irritation
kUrta	a sort of dress
kUlhi	a sort of cap
kUlphi	a sort of cup
kUlle	all
kŨər	lovely son
kŨwar	unmarried
kŨwari	unmarried (f.)
kŨwã	well
kũs	a sort of hay
kuṭ	press
kUṭni	politician, and a wicked woman
ke	who, of
kekro	of any one
kekkər	whom
ketəna	how much
kela	banana
kes	hair
kesIya	hair
koa	palm fruit
koṭhəri	room
kotahi	miserliness
kotbali	police-station
korIək phul	a sort of flower
kora	raw
korsis	try
kosIs	try
kose	to blame
koṛhi	leper
kə͜i	how many, vomiting
kə͜ĩa	miser
kə͜ia	moss
kə͜io	so many
kə͜ik	many

kə͜il	have done
kə͜ilək	done
kə͜ilas	a name
kə͜i+las	how may dead bodies?
kə͜ise	how
kə͜isən	how
ka͜ĩ	a sort of noise
ko͜i	any one
ko͜ĩa	a kind of leaf vegetable
ko͜ia	inner part of palm fruit
ko͜i+a	any one come
ko͜ila	coal
ko͜i+la	take any one
ku͜ĩa	well
ku͜ĩe	well
ku͜ĩo	even well
kə͜uwa	crow
kə͜un	who
kə͜unIa	pieces of grain
kiul	a place-name
kẽuṛa	orange, a sort of flower

kh

khə̃jri	a sort of musical instrument
khəjur	a sort of dry fruit,
khəṭṭa	sour
khəṭola	small cot
khəṭbaspəṭbas	the bed
khəṭməl	a bed-bug
khən	dig
khənḍa	ornament, artical
khənḍha	house garden
khəmira	seasoned
khəmbha	pol
khər	much fried
khəṛa	stand up
khərab	bad
khərid lū	I have purchased
khərra	fair
khə̃ṛhər	remains
kha	eat
khaja	a kind of sweet
kha+ja	please eat
khatIr	for
khan	mine
khaṭ	cot
kham	I would eat
khal	have eaten
kha lə	please eat
khala	mother's sister
kha+la	please eat
khas	special
khIə͜ila	decayed
khĩc	draw
khir	pudding with rice and milk
khUrpi	sickle
khUs	happy
khub	much
khubsurət	beautiful
khur	hoof
khet	field
khel	to play
khõta	nest
khõtəbe	nest

kho	eat
khojəte	in searching
khojəm	I would search or find out
khojəl	found
khoje	to search
khoje la	for search
kholke	after opening
khəiəi	would I eat?
khəiəu	would I eat?
khəitəi	he will eat
khəir	well, good position
khəilə̃	have you taken your meal?
khəile	have you taken your meal?
Khəiləkəi	had he meal?
khai	to eat
khaila	for eating
khoie	outer part of fruit
khoicha	a bundle of presentation in sari
kheu	rowing

g

gəcea	dig
gəchIya	plant
gəccno	accept
gəḍḍha	ditch
gənga	the biggest river of India, Ganga
gənj	a place
gənḍa	the number of four
gəndh	smell
gəp	gossip
gəph	thick
gəbbər	deaf
gəmcha	country made toble
gəmla	an earten pot in which flowers can be put in
gəṛ	bury
gəṛhna	to be built
gəya	a famous holy place of Hindus
gərəj	purpose
gərI	the inner material of coconut
gərib	poor
gəllũ	would I suffer?
gəs	faint
ga	sing
gā̃ṭh	knot
gath	to be thread
gan	song
gani	wise
gabhIn	pregnant animal
gaṛi	cart
garũ	would I squeegee
gal	sung
gahĩ	sing
gahi	a numeral
gIyan	knowledge
gIrəl	got down
gIrja	a name of a girl
gIr+ja	fall down
gIrhəst	a man of family

gIrhəsti	life of a family
git	song
gidh	eagle
guccha	bunch
gUrəba	a name
gUrU	teacher
gUlla	a small piece of suger cane
gũth	to tie
gUni	qualified
gẽd	football
gendri	worthless clothes
gel	went
gelən	have gone
gelIəu	went
gelo	has he gone?
gelə͜i	went
gelha	stone of a fruit
gehũ	wheat
gokUl	a famous place
gotIarI	kinship
gotni	sister-in-law
godna	tattoo
gor	fair complexion
gossa	anger
ga͜i	cow
ga͜ib	disappear
gə͜u	cow
gə͜ua	cow
gə̃͜ua	village
gə̃͜ue	village
gə͜una	second marriage
gə͜u+na	not cow
gə͜urəb	greatness
ga͜u	sing
gã͜u	village

gh

ghəṭna	incident
ghə̃ghəra	a sort of petticoat
ghəmci	prickly heat
ghər	house
ghər-dUar	house & door
ghərbali	wife
ghərelu	which belongs to home
ghəṛi	watch, time
ghãs	grass
ghaṭa	loss
ghan	ill fame
ghIyahI	which is made with ghee
ghIr	to be surrounded
ghi	ghee
ghiyo	even ghee
ghUr	turn back
ghŨs	to rush in
ghur	turn up
ghere	surround
ghor	much
ghoṛsəbar	horse rider
ghəila	earthen water pot
gha͜il	wounded
ghe͜ud	cluster of fruits
ghə͜ur	bunch
ghi͜u	ghee
ghi͜ua	ghee

c

cəkəla	pastry-board

cəkta	spot
cətUr	wise
cənkəl	broken
cənədərgUpt	name of a famous empror
cənnən	sandal wood
cəpṭa	disfigured
cãpa	accident
cəpra	a kind of Lakh
cəmkə	be bright
cəmkəl	brightened
cəmpa	a sort of flower
cəṛIt	character
cərUa	water pot
cərkha	a sort of wheel
cərbi	fat
cəl	walk
cələt	walk
cələl	having walked
cələte	walked
cəlabe	to moove
cəlabela	for maintenance for start
cəlãk	clever
cəlãki	cleverness
cəlna	to go
cəlt na	don't go
cəska	habit
cəsma	optical
cãndni	moon light
can	moon
canək	the great politician of ancient India
car	four
cara cUgge la for feeding	
cah	desire
cahi	should
cahã hã	do you want?
cahlək	wished, wanted
cIṭhIya	letter
cIta	funeral pyre
cIpəṭ	catch up
cIṛəĩ	bird
cIṛyã	bird
cIṛəiyã	bird
cicUai	sweating
cij	thing
cit	lay down on back
cita	tiger
cir	cut
cũr	joint of a cot
cu	leak
cur	press
cue	let it leak
cuəi	let it leak
cuəu	let it leak
cUkIya	earthen toys
cUkka	small earthen pot
cUg	to finish
cUgge	to eat
cun	twisted cloth
cum kər	after kissing
cuṛi	bracelet
cur	press
cUpcap	silent
cUɒpe	silent
cUllU	handful

cõ	a sort of sound
cõdhIya	brighten
coṭi	peak
cobh	suck
cə͜it	a month of spring (caitra)
cə͜in	relief
ca͜ĩ	seed
ca͜i	tea
cə͜ue	the four fingers
cə͜ukənna	aware
cə͜ukIdari	the work of night guard
cə͜ura	rice
cə͜uwa	the four fingers

ch

chəṭpṭal	suffered from pain
chətIya	heart
chəppər	roof made with earthen and bamboo article
chəbo	six of them
chəl	cheat
chəlke	over lapping of water
chəl+ke	having deceived
chati	heart
chan	roof
chIp	disguise
chik	sneeze
chu	touch
chuə	please touch
chuye	touch
chura	dagger
ched	hole
choṭkI	younger (f.)
choṛ	leave
choṛ ke	left
choṛbə͜u	I shall leave
chu͜iə͜i	would I touch?
chU͜iə͜u	would I touch?
cha͜ũ	shade
cha͜u	dramatic action
chẽ͜u	news of goodness
che͜u	cut

J

jəg	the world
jəgəhpər	on the place,
jəgələ͜i	arose
jəggəl	risen
jəngəl	forest
jəngəlIo	even forest
jəntri	a sort of superstitious thing
jənni	woman
jənmla	please take birth
jəpt	confiscated
jəb	while
jəbab	answer
Jəbahər	a kind of dimond
jəbahIrat	precious stones
jərə	please burn
jəra	some what

jərur	sure
jərda	a variety of tobacco
jəl	burn, water
jəlabə	burn
jələ͜ilək	burnt
jələm	birth
jəlabəm	to fire
jəlməl	born
jəs	fame
jəhã	any where, world
jəhã̄gir	a name of an emperor
ja	go
jake	having gone
jãgh	thigh
jãce	to examine
jat	caste
jat həl	to go
jan	know
jane	know
jane la	for knowing
jane ləgi	for knowing
jam	a sort of cup
jamUn	a sort of small black fruit
jare	to be burnt
jal	net
jahã	are you going?
jaha	please tell, are your going?
jahĩ	go
jahe	(he) goes
jahə͜i	(he) goes
jId	persistence
jInora	a kind of crop
ji	alive
jiə	live long
jia	heart
ji+a	live long
jiə͜i	live long
jibən	life
jibh	tongue
jŨar	a sort of physical reaction
jUanI	youth
jugnU	night worm
jUtta	shoe
juwa	gamble
jUwan	young
jUṛba	fever, twin
je	who
jekəra	which
jəkəra se	by which
jekkər	its
jo	go
jõk	a sort of water insect
jõkh	chance
jog	chance
jə͜i	victory
jə͜ibə͜u	would I go?
jə͜isən	like
je͜isehi	as soon as
ja͜i	he may go
ja͜ila	for going
ji͜uwa	creature
jə̃͜ua	twin
jã͜u	go
juo	even gamble

jh

jhəkh	to be irritated
jhəpkəl	dozen
jhəmar	insult
jhər	give up
jhan	sad
jhUnḍ	group
jhUmka	a sort of earning
jhUrri	wrinkle
jhõk	speed
jhopəṛi	hut
jhopəṛiya	hut
jhor	curry

ṭ

ṭəg	to move
ṭəṭəka	fresh
ṭəpke	to fall
ṭəp+ke	after crossing
ṭar	neglect
ṭImṭIm	twinkle
tUkəli	a small disk
ṭUṭəlka	broken
ṭon	a sort of sound
ṭunṭUn meṭUn	a sort of sound
ṭuər	orhən
ṭola	small part of a village

ṭh

ṭhəg	cheat
ṭhənke	to be thundered
ṭhən+ke	with full speed
ṭhəri	standing
ṭhərra	a kind of skin disease, rough wine
ṭhəs	weak
ṭhan	decesion
ṭhik	fixed
ṭhIkana	place, address
ṭhIṭhək	stop a while
ṭhika	contract
ṭhekua	a kind of sweet
ṭhok	beat
ṭhokbəjake	after well examination

ḍ

ḍəg	step
ḍənk	beat
ḍəbbha	raw coconut
ḍər	fear
ḍərabe	to show fear
ḍəs	bit
ḍabh	green coconut
ḍar	branch of a tree
ḍal	branch of a tree
ḍĨg	boast
ḍIg	slack
ḍIbba	small box
ḍIrar	line
ḍol	to fluctuate

ḍh

ḍhəkəna	cover of a pot
ḍhəg	loose
ḍhər	to be kindly
ḍhəlŨa	slopy

ḍhəlUa	drunkard
ḍhəhəl	destroyed
ḍhal	shield
ḍhIbra	name of a village
ḍhIlli	loose (f.)
ḍhUlmUl	which is not fixed
ḍhːəu̯o	even coin

t

tə	then
tək	till
təgədir	fate
təjjUb	wonder
təb	then
təbna	to be heated
təbla	a musical instrument
tərəhra	ditch
tərəh	sort, kind
təraju	an article of measurment, a scale
tərkib	method
tələk	to the extent
təlUk	meanwhile
təsbir	photo, a portrait
təsbIːIya	photo, a portrait
təsla	a sort of pot
tatəl	hot
tan	to be tighten
tar	telegram
tItki	a spark of fire
tInko	even a piece
tiyag	leave
tIləuri	pudding made of seeds
tIrsul	a sort of weapon
tire	side of river
tisra	third
tUrte	soon
tũ	you
teag	sacrifice
tel	oil
teli	oilman
tõ	you
to	then
totəṛaha	stammerer
tor	your
tora	you
təiyar	ready
toi	lace
teus	last third year

th

thək	tired
thak	layer
than	a sort of measurment
thal	dish
thali	dish
thUkni	woman who spits much
thoṛa	some, a little
thoṛIke	little
thoṛi der	some time

d

dəbaho	press

dəmahi	a performance of agriculture
dəya	compassion
dərəd	pain
dərojja	the interance room of house
dərmaha	monthly salary
dəs	ten
dəsa	condition
dəsIe	maid servant
dəhəjəl	teased
dəhin	kindfull
da	give
dan	donation
dab	press
dam	cost
dami	costly
dasi	maid servant
dIk	disturbance
dIn	day
dIne	days
dInma	day
dIyar	sandy land within a river
dIlcəspi	interest
dIlbo	even heart
dIyasəla͜i	match box
dio	may I give?
didi	sister
din	day
diya	earthen lamp
dUkh	grief
dUkhIt	disturbed, sufferer
dUkhIya	sufferer

dUkhi	sufferer
dUtkar	chide
dUnIyã	world
dUnnU	both
dUnhũ	both
dUnhũ ke	of both
dUwar	door
dUwari	door
dUsəmən	enemy
duəri	door
dukan	shop
du+kan	two ears
dugo	two
dur	far
durho	get out
duho	suck milk
de	give
deke	after giving
dekh	see
dekhə	please see
dekha	please see
dekhəl kə͜i	visitors
dekhəte	seeing
dekhətahər	visitors
dekhələk	saw
diyara	a sandy land within a river
dekhũ	let me see?
det	give
dena	to give
dem	I shall give
dema	will you give?
der	delay
del	already given
delək	gave

delkə͜i	gave
delthIn	gave
dewər	husband's younger brother
desba	country
dehIya	body
dehĩ	give
dehi	body
deho	please give
dost	friend
dosər	next one
dohəba	verse
dohər	a thick-rapper
də͜iya	sister
də͜uṛ	to run
dəuṛəl	run
de͜ur	husband's brother
de͜ura	husband's brother

dh

dhən	money
dhənmə͜iti	name of a girl
dhəpla	trick
dhəmkabe	to show fear
dhər	put down
dhərba	current
dhərna	stage satyagrah
dhərohər	subject of prestige
dhərhəra	remaining parts
dhan	paddy
dham	sacred place
dhIya	children
dhIrəj	petience
dhUn me	in the purpose
dhu͜ĩa	smoke
dhu͜ə̃il	smoked
dhu͜ə̃i	let it to be smoked
dho	wash
dho͜ə	please wash
dho əl	washed
dhoa	a name of a river, please wash
dho͜e	let to be washed
dhoa͜u	wash
dhokha se	by cheating
dhotIya	a garment
dhobi	washer-man
dho la	please wash

n

nə	no
nəkṭi	nose dirt
nəkkəl	caricature
nəg	costly stone
nəjər	glance
nəjdik	near
nəṭka	dwarf
nəṭni	tale bearer (woman)
nətIya	motherly grandson
nəthIya	nose ring
nədIya	river
nəddi	river
nənIya	motherly grand mother

nənna	motherly grand father
nəppa	measurment
nəbbəl	downed
nəmuna	specimen
nəmuno	even specimen
nəmkin	salty
nəmma	name
nəya	new
nələnda	name of a famous learning centre
nəs	vain, to be impure
nəsəl	impure
nəsa͜i	to be impure
nəha͜i	bath
nəhə͜ite	during bath
nəha͜ila	for bath
na	no
nag	the king of snake
nagIn	the queen of snake
naj	pride
nadh	start
nap	measurment
nam	name
nar	woman
nIar	presentation
nIklə	please to be out
nIkəl	to get out
nIklə	please to be out
nIkəl ke	after getting out
nIkale	take out
nIkal lək	taken out
nIkallũ	I took out
nIkal ke	after taking out
nIkləl	kept out
nIkəl pəṛəl	which has came out
nIcce	below
nimək	salt
nIrṃəl	pure
nĩlar	forehead
nIhəcə͜i	dicision
niar	presentation
nigori	a bad name
nipəl	washed
nipte	having washed
nind	sleeping
niyət	intension
nila	a colour
nihUr	bent
nUka	to conceal
neta	leader
nebari	hay
newar	a kind of big lace
neyar	presentation of sweet
noc	snatching
noskha	prescription
nə͜i	no
nə͜ie	boat
nə͜ito	otherwise
nə͜u	nine
nə͜ukər	servant
nə͜ukranIỹa	maid servant
na͜u	put down or boat
ne͜u	foundation

ne͜uta	invitation
ne͜ur	mangose
ni͜uwa	foundation

p

pəkəṛ	catch
pəkka	floor
pə̃kh	feather
pəkh	a fort night
pəgha	rope
pəcbəjna	a traditional musical set
pəchətabe	repentance
pəcchIm	west
pəṭṭə	adjustment
pəṭṭi	bandage
pəṭṭha	strong
pəta	address
pətta	leaf
pətthər	rock
pətra	the book of astronomy
pətla	lean and thin
pənkh	feather
pənkhi	feather
pənc	a group of five
pəncər	leaked
pənchi	bird
pənja	five fingers
pənḍa	who conducts the religious performance
pən tal	rice of water
pənth	way
pənala	drainage
Pənpnal	sharply, angry
pənsokkha	rainbow
pərətIgỹa	oath
pəran	life
pərathəna	pray
pərani	person
pərta	adjustment
pəribar	family
pərba	the last performance, to flow in water
pərbes	enter
pərna	a religious performance
pəror	a kind of vegetable
pər	but
pərem	love
pəṛ	fall
pəṛəl	fallen
pəṛələ͜i	fell down
pəṛələ͜i	fell
pəṛna	to fall
pəṛgel	fallen
pə̃ṛkI	a kind of small bird
pəṛos	neighbouring
pəṛh	read
pəṛhələkə͜i	read
pəṛhe	reading
pəṛhəbə	to teach
pəlthi	to sit cross legged
pəlna	cradle
pə̃ləni	name of a village

pəsənd	like
pəsij gel	to be moved
pəsena	sweat
pə̃sga	a sort of weight
pəsrəl	spread
pəhəlban	a wrestler
pəhəṛba	hill
pəhaṛ	hill
pəhIla	the first one
pəhIlese	from the begining
PəhUc	reach, approach
pəhŨcəl	reached
pəhcan	recognise
pãka	mud
pãcõ	five
pach	acratch
paṭha	he goat
padri	christian padri
pan	betel leaf
pani	water
panc səu̯	five hundred
par	cross
para	murcury
pari	chance
pare	on the other side of river
paro	popular name for girls
palək	a kind of vegetable
pale pose	serve, preserve
pas	near, net
pĩe	drink
pIət	drink
pIəri	yellow cloth
pIəl	drunk
pĨjəṛa	cage
piche	back
pIchUəṛba	backside of house
pInpIn	weeping
pIyas	thirsty
pIye	drink
pIyar	love
pi	drink
piət	drink
piu̯	lover or husband
pia	lover or husband
pi+a	please drink
pĩak	drunkard
pitri	he will drink
piṛha	a small seat of wood
piye	drink
piyer	yellow
piri	yellow
pis	press
pUchlək	asked
pUttUl	puppet
pUtna	a name
pUwar	hay
pura	complete
pure	whole
peṭ	stomach
pẽrəl	dissatisfied
poar	hay
pokha	a sort of small fruit
porsa	a measurement of depth

pə͜i	charge
pə͜ire	swim
pə͜isa	a sort of small coin
pa͜i	get
po͜ĩa	a kind of vegetable
po͜ia	baby snake
pə̃͜ua	feet
pə̃͜ua	a measurement
pi͜ũ	shall I drink?
pi͜u	lover or husband

ph

phə̃s	engage
phəgUwa	a festival of Hindus
phətte	a name
phen	hood
phənela	fig
phənda	net
phəndhəba	net
phəl	result, fruit
phãk	a piece of fruit
phan	jump
phaltu	redundant, irrelevant
phikir	grief
phIkka	tasteless
phInU	again
phInU se	again
phĩc	wash
phŨhĨ	raining in drops
phUnsi	pimple
phUṭ gel	open
phUlə͜ule	to be out of mood
phUhər	energetic
phũk	blow
phul	flower
phulpUr	name of a village
phŨṭ	enmity
phẽk	throw
phẽku	which is thrown
phẽkə͜u	would he throw?
phokca	water bowl

b

bəkə͜in	impotent cow
bəksa	box
bəkhet	time
bəkheṛa	complication
bəkhori	a lower cast
bəkhətIyarkhIlji	a name
bəgeri	a kind of small bird
bəgə͜irəh	etc.
bəgghi	a traditional vehicle
bəca	safe
bəca le	to save
bəcchər	year
bəcba	chicken
bəcbə͜u	live
bəjəh	cause
bəjərIya	market
bəjjhəl	engaged
bəjkəl	rotten
bəḍ	very
bəḍh	grow

bəḍhIya	flood
bətə͜ilthIn	told
bətə͜ilək	told
bəta	tell
bəteə͜ibə͜u	I will speak
bədən	body
bədle	on the place of
bədra	cloud
bədla	revenge
bədhIya	religious thread
bən ke	being made
bən gel	became
bəncər	fool, uncivilised
bənd	close
bəndri	she-monkey
bənabe la	for designing
bənba	make
bən ber	a kind of fruit
bəbul	gum tree
bəmtal	out of control
bemtaha	whimsical
bərə	feel
bərərI	celling
bərabri	similarity
bərahəmən	brahmin
bərali	a place
bər	bridegroom
bərkəl	decayed
bərcha	a kind of sharp arm
bərna	but, to burn
bərphi	a sort of sweet
bərma	a sort of needle
bərIs	year
bərsat	rainy season
bərha	number of twelve
bəṛəhə͜iya	carpenter
bəṛIya	garden
bəṛẽṛ	wooden ceiling
bəṛki	younger girl
bəṛhIỹa	better
bəṛhi	carpenter
bəṛhe	forward
bələ	please burn
bəla	trouble
bəIUrĩ	remaining part
bəlkha͜i	fluctuate
bəlmə͜iti	name of a girl
bəlrI	insubstantial part
bəs	stop
bəsənt	spring season
bəsəl	established
bəsUrI	flute
bəsul	paid
bəsphəṭṭa	a thin and small form of bamboo
bəhə	please flow
bəhəl	being flown
bəha	flow
bəhana	false talk
bəhI	account book
bəhInIyã	sister
bəhU	daughter-in-law
bəhUt sa	so many
bəheli	bird catcher
bak	sentence
baki	credit
bagh	tiger

bac	read
bach	sorting out
bacha	calf
baj	time to time, pigeon
bãjh	impotent woman
bajh	pigeon
baṭ	way
baḍh	growth
bat	matter
batcit	talk
bad	after
bãdh	to make as a knot
badh	exclude
badhũ	would I bind?
ban	arrow
bap	father
bapəs	come back
bapIs	come back
bape	father
babu	father, big boss
bar	day
barəh	twelve
bare	scrifice, to burn
baṛh	flood
bal	hair
bala	golden bracelet
bal gopal	children
balbəcca	children
balŨ	would I put on?
balu	sand
bãs	bamboo
bas	residence
bIkkəl	sold
bIkh	poison
bIgəṛ	destroyed, angry
bIgUl	a sort of whistle
bIcar	consideration
bIcca	seed
bIjog	separation
bIjjhəl	rotten
bItte	spend
bIdana	pomegrenate
bĨdh	a famous mountain
bIdh	rules regulations
bIn	without
bInan	knitting
bInal	woven
bIpət	trouble
bIman	airplane
bImari	disease
bIyakUl	restless
bIyan	birth
bIyana	advance money
bIyaban	deserted place
bIyah	marriage
bIyahi ə͜urət	married woman
bIl	hole
bIlkUl	complete
bIlap	weeping
bIsar	leave
bIsṭI	underwear
bisbas	faith
bĨhən	seeds
bIa͜i	let her give birth
biog	separation
bidore	disfigured
bin	a musical instrument

birbəl	name of a man
bihən	seed
bucc	earless
bIUḍḍha	oldman
bUtəru	boy
bUrUs	brush
bUṛbək	fool
bUṛhIya	old woman
bUl	walk
bu	smell
bua	father's sister
buṛha	old man
bec	sell
becara	poor fellow (he)
becari	poor fellow (she)
becŨ	would I sell?
bece	sell
beṭa	son
beṭasəbh	sons
beṭIə͜uri	which belongs to girl on the occasion of marriage
beṭi	girl
bẽt	cane
beni	braid
bel	a sort of fruit
bela	time
belə͜uwa	name of a place
belba	time, a sort of fruit
belna	a rolled tool of kitchen
behal	eager
bokU	fool

bogca	worthless things
bodda	fool
bol	speak
bolə	speak
boləl	spoken
bolək	spoke
boləlkə͜i	spoke
boli	speech
bole	to speak
bol lə͜i	spoke
boləl	spoke
bolaba	please call
bolə͜i	to speak
bole	tell
bolabela	for calling
bolake	having called
bolabhelək	sent to call
bolta	soul
bolti	soul
bə͜iṭh	sit down
bə͜iṭhə	please sit down
bə͜iṭhIə͜u	would i sit down?
bə͜iṭhna	to sit
bə͜id	doctor
bəil	ox
bəina	presentation
ba͜ĩ	left
ba͜i	wind of stomach
ba͜il	outsider
bu͜i	a subject of fear
bu͜ia	a subject of fear
bə͜ual	misled
bə͜u au	let him dream
bə͜u͜ai	let him to be

	dreamed
bə͜udh	the followers of Lord Buddha
bə͜ut	device

bh

bhəgət	devotee
bhəgəban	God
bhəgəbano	even God
bhəgṭha	hurdle
bhənḍa	secret
bhənḍar	store
bhər	fill up
bhər peṭ	completely
bhərme	whole
bhəla	a sort of speech
bhãg	a sort of intoxicating thing
bhag	fly away
bhagəl	flew away
bhãj	obstruction
bhaph	steam
bhan	feel
bhari	heavy
bhIkhəmənga	begger
bhIchusəb	followers of Lord Buddha
bhi	also
bhikh	begging
bhir	near
bhũe	earth
bhuo	let it to be rotten
bhua͜u	let it to be rotten
bhut	ghost
bhej	send
bhel	happened
bhẽr	sheep
bhõkəl	stabbed
bhojən	meal
bhothər	which is not sharp
bhə͜i	fear
bhə͜iya	brother
bhã͜i	a fearful sound
bha͜i	brother
bhuiyã	earth
bha͜u	rate
bhũo	even earth

m

məkhana	a dry fruit
məkkhən	butter
məgədhIyn	people of Magadh
məgər	but
məgji	lace
məcIya	country made easy chair
məchəlI	fish
məjədUri	labour/payment
məjəbur	forced, helpless
məṭkəl	walk at ease
məṭṭha	butter milk
mət	no, don't
məth	to churn
məd	purpose
mədət	help
mədh	honey
mən	mind

mənemən	in mind
mənke	of mind
mənjur	accept
mənjer	blooms
mənjha	a kind of paste for thread
məntri	minister
mənd	slow
mər	die
mərəd	man, husband
mərəlka	died
məraṭha	people of Maharashtra
mərji	choice
məror	stomach pain
məṛora	stomach pain
məṛai	hut
məlal	complaint
məlka	queen, lightning
məlba	cup for oil
məllah	fisher
məst	happyful
məsan	graveyard
məsjId	the prayer place of Mohammdans
məsəhur	famous
məhməh	a sort of smelling
məhək	smell
məhəl	palace
məhatma	saint
məhina	month
məhino	months
məhInna	month
məhoba	a historical place
m̃ag	beg
maghī	which belongs to a month of winter
matha	head
majəl	washed
majhəl	pasted, younger one
man	accept, prestige
manu	woul I accept?
mane	meaning
manoməṛjad	prestige
maphi	excuse
marphət	through
mar	beat
maṛ	water of rice
mal	goods
malum	to know
malomal	rich
malkIn	mistress
mah	month
mIl	meet
mI lə	please meet
mIləl	found
mIle	find
mijh	to put off (light)
mItəba	friend
mir	the first one
mUnga	a sort of vegetable
mUr	turn
mUrad	choice
mUrgi	hen, chiken
mUrjhal	fade up
mUrti	emage
mUrda	dead body

mUhə kan	mouth and ear
mur	capital
mul	rooṭ
muh	mouth
me	in
mear	name a of village
megh	rain
mer	a set, similarity
mel	similarity, symmetry
mehətər	sweeper
mehənət	labour
moch	mustache
mor	peacock
more	my, mine
mol	cost
mom	wax
moṛha	table
mə͜ia	mother
mə͜ina	a kind of bird
mə͜il	dirt
ma͜i	mother
mə͜uj	merriment
mə͜uji	jovial
mə͜ur	a sort of crown to be worn in marriage

r

rəkhe	to have
rəkhlək	had
rejkŨwar	prince
rəjkŨwari	princess
rətĩya	night
rənIa	queen
rənIyn	queen's
rənk	poor, begger
rəng	colour
rənj	anger
rə̃ṛIya	a sort of bad name
rəs	juice
rəsta	way
rəh	remain
rəhə	please live
rəhe	live, remain
rəhə͜i	live
rəhəl	lived
rəhgel	lived
rəhəle	live
rəhəlo	live
rəhlə͜i	live
rakh	ash
raj	kingdom
raja	king
raje	king, kingdom
rajkŨwari	princess
rajməhəl	palace
rat	night
rani	queen
ras	a kind of religious play
rIyaj	habit
rIwaj	custom
rua	cotton
ru͜iba	cotton
rUpə͜iya	coins
re	a sort of address
reai	concession
rẽk	rough vioce

rẽt	cut
ret	sand
reḍIo	radio
resma	name of a girl
resmi	silken
rehu	a kind of fish
ro	weep
ro͜e	let him weep
ro͜əi	let him weep
ro͜aĩ	weeping
ro͜ĩ	a sort of sound
ro͜i	let him weep
ro͜iə͜u	would I weep?
roəl	weept
rog	disease
roj	daily
rojəgar	business
roji	maintenance, capital business
roṭi	bread
rob	impression
robə	weep
roba͜i	weeping
rohIt	name of boy

I

ləkəṛi	charcoal
ləkəṛIya	charcoal
ləkba	paralysis
ləkkhəl	seen, found
ləgəl	attached
ləgəhəl	attached
ləgələn	experienced
ləga	attached
ləgi	for
ləgə͜ile	attach, put on
ləgga	long stick
ləgba	big stick
ləglə͜i	felt
ləcka	a traditional conveyance
ləcchən	feature
ləjal	being shield
ləṭpəṭ	unfair (behaviour)
ləḍUwa	a kind of round sweet
ləḍḍu	a kind of round sweet
lətchUt	infection
ləddəl	loaded
lənṭh	fool
lənḍ	vulger word for penis
lənḍha	without tale
ləbdhəl	clung
ləmba	long
ləbni	an earthen pot
ləbṛa	tale bearer
ləmna	an earthen pot
ləmni	an earthen pot
ləmpha	laltern
ləmri	tener
ləmhər	tall
ləlki	red coloured
ləlcəl	greedy
lələcte	in greeding
ləpeṭke	after binding
ləpeṭəl	wound
ləṛ	fight

ləṛki	girl
ləṛəkən	children
ləṛəkpən	childhood
ləṛUwa	a round sweet of rice flower
ləssa	attraction
la	for
lagəl	fixed, attached
lãghəl	crossed
laj	shyness
ladəl	loaded
labəl	brought
labh	gain
lal	a precious stone, red
lIkh	write
lIkhəl	written
lIyakət	capacity
li͜əũ	would I take?
likh	the insect of hair
lila	play of God
lUgai	wife
lUcca	wicked, untruthful
le	take
leə͜au	bring
leke	having
lekha	writing
legelə͜i	took
lekIn	but
let	take
lete	taking
labe	take
lebe la	for taking
lem	I will take
lelək	took
lelkə͜i	took
lelelək	catch, took
lelthIn	took, got
lemu	lemon
lehũ	I take
lehu	blood
log	people
loṭ	down
loṛh	gather
lohərba	blacksmith
loha	iron, challange
lohar	blacksmith
lohe	iron
lə͜i	paste
lo͜ial	being rounded
lo͜iya	a round shape
lə͜u	flame
lə͜uṭ	came back
lə͜uṛi	maid servant
la͜ũ	would I bring it?

s

səkət	can
səkəl	could
səktI	strength
səkhətI	hardness
səkhIya	girl friend
səkhi	girl friend
səkht	hard
səga͜i	marriage, second marriage
səc	true
səcce	true
səcce me	really

səjjəl	decorated
səṭhIya	sixty years old
sətela	step (m)
sətsəng	symposium
səttu	a sort of flour
səḍharən	ordinary
səḍhUwan	nun
sənkh	conchshell
sənkha	conchshell
sənkər	Lord Siva
Səng	with
Səngh	association
səngmərmer	marble
sənjha	of evening
sənjo	to preserve
sənṭ	neglect
sənḍh	one who eats much
səntokh se	with satisfaction
səntos	satisfaction
sənt	saint
səntra	orange
səntri	guard
sənthal	a tribe
sənal	over
sənyas	life of saint
səpər	think, plan
səpna	dream
səphIya	clearner
sə̃pəha	where snake lives
səphər	travelling
səb	all
sə̃bə̃r	decorate
səbək	lesson

səbari	vehicle
səbere	early in the morning
səbur	satisfaction
səburi	satisfaction
səbja	green colour
səbh	all
sə̃bhal	aware
səbhe	all
səməjh	think, understand
səməjh bujh ke	after understanding
səməjhlək	understand
səmjhəni hən	understood
səməjhbə͜i	I shall understand
səmet	along with
səmə͜i	time
səmau	insert
səmṭha	thick stick
sərkaro	even government
sərahe	praise
sərIya	decorate a sort of plant
sərir	body
sərtha	name of a village
sərdha	affection
sə̃rṣĨ	tongs
səwar	decorate
səlam	a sort of wish
səltal	calm
sə̃sta	cheep
səsuar	father-in-las's house

səɦər	city
səhej	preserve
səhur	wiseness, manner
sãjh	evening
sãjhe	evening
saj	decorate
sajh	honest
saṭna	to paste
sat	seven
satəgo	seven
sato	seven
sath	with
sathisəb	friends
sadi	marriage
san	dignity
saph	clear
samne	in front of
sami	hunband
sãs	breath
sas	mother-in-law
sar	substance
saro	name of a girl
saya	petticoat
sahu	a sirname
sĨyar	fox
sIkca	shackle
sIkkh	a religious community
sIgreṭ	cigarette
sInthu	name of a village
sImṭəl	restricted
sIyan	stitching
sIwan	name of a place
sīk	stab
siə	stitch
sia	sita
siət	stitch
sit	dew
sib	an insect of river
simbh	a sort of vegetable
sibu	a name
sir	head
siṛhi	stair case
sUərəg	heaven
sUkh	happy
sUkhəni	name of a woman
sUkhəle	for drying
sUkhənt	to be dried
sUjog	chance
sUtlə	sleep
sUttəl	slept
sUtte	sleep
sUtlo	sleep
sUn	hear
sUnke	being heard
sUnlək	heard
sUnḍh	an insect of rice
sUnnər	beautiful
sUrUkərlək	began
sUrendər	a name
sUṛkəl	sipped
sUṛUp	sip
sua	big needle
suog	chance
suər	swine
sut	thread

sur	blind, mood
suṛhi	a caste
se	to, with
seṭh	rich man
sẽt	preserve
senUria	reddish
seba	service
ser	lion, a measurement
sehət	health
sehi se	for that reason
sõc	think
sõcə	please think
soakhən	welcome
sõcte	thinking
sõclək	thought
sot	sources of water
sona	gold
sonar	goldsmith
sobab	test
sobhab	nature
sobha͜u	nature
sõph	a sort of spices
sor	sources of water
sõs	crocodile
sos	to be end
sohag	fortune of a woman
sohaga	a sort of a mineral
sohagi	fortunate girl
soha͜i	like
sə̃͜ia	lover, husband
sə͜ia	bed
so͜i	sources of water
so͜ia	sources of water
so͜io	do I sleep
so͜iə͜i	would I sleep?
su͜i	needle
su͜ia	needle
sə͜u	hundred
sə̃͜use	whole
sa͜u	a sirname
sĩ͜u	would I stitch?
si͜u	Lord Siva
sẽ͜u	to serve
se͜u	apple
se͜ue	apple
se͜uo	even apple

h

hə̃ka͜u	call
həkIə͜u	I am
həkim	doctor
həkə͜i	is
həḍIya	bone
həḍḍa	lean and thin
həḍḍi	bone
həṭIya	village market
həṭhəba	persistency
həṭhIya	persistency
hənḍha	day light
həns	swan
həpta	week
həba	air
həm	I, myself
həmərа	my, me
həmmər	my, mine
həmme	I, myself
həmto	I

həmnisəbh	ourself
həmhi	myself
hər	every, take up
həre	please take up
həra	green
hərIəri	greenness
hərre	a sort of herb
həṛIya	earthen pot
həl	was
hə̃la	was
hələ͜i	was
həlthIn	was
həldi	turmeric
həsi	laughter
həsUli	heavy necklace
hə̃se	to laugh
hə̃sə͜i	to laugh, ill fame
hã	yes
ha	alas!
hath	hand
han	ill fame
hãph	throbbing
har	defeat, garland
haṛ	bone
hal	news
halət	condition
hIə͜i	is
hIkmət	device
hĨḍol	swing
hInkər	his
hInkha	his, him
hInkhe	his, him
hIndu	a nation, cast
hĨya	here
hĨyã se	from here
hĨrsa	competition
hĨṛor	acute pain of stomach
hIlmIlke	happily, united
hĩ	is
hĩe	here
hia͜u	carriage
hĩg	a sort of spices
hin	inferior
hũe	there
hUḍUk	the action of plunge
hUnər	art
hUyã	there
hUrra	blow
hUṛUk	swallaw
hUlaṛ	fox, cat
hũ	yes
huhu	a sort of sound
he	is
hɔ	become, happen
hoə͜u	let it happen
hot	happen, become
hobə	become
hol	happened
holo	happened, became
holə͜i	became, happened happened
hosIyar	clever
hə͜i	is
ha͜i	alas!
hə͜u	is

BIBLIOGRAPHY

Allen, W.S. *Phonetics in Ancient India*, Oxford, 1953.

Armstrong and Ward, Eda C. *A Handbook of English Intonation*, Cambridge, 1949.

Artemov, Vladimir. Tone and Intonation, Proceedings of the Fourth International Congress of Phonetic Sciences, 1961.

Aryani, Sampatti. *Magahi Vyakaran kosh*, Patna, 1965.

Bahri, Hardeo. *Lahndi Phonetics*, Allahabad, 1963.

Bloch,Bernard & George, L.Trager. *Outline of Linguistic Analysis,* Baltimore, 1949.

Bloomfield, L. *Language,* India, 1963.

Brite, William. *Bharat Ki Bhashayon me Mahapran Byanjan Hindi Anushilan*, Dhirendra Verma Visheshank, Allahabad, 1960.

Census Commissioner. Census of India, Language Volume, New Delhi, 1951.

Chatterji, S.K. A Sketch of "Bengali Phonetics", *B.S.O.A.S.* Vol.II, Part I, 1961.

——, *Indo-Aryan and Hindi,* Calcutta, 1960.

Chiba, T. and Kajiyama, M. *The Vowels, Its Nature and Structure*, Tokyo, 1958.

Diwakar, R.R. *Bihar Through the Ages,* patna, 1958.

Fairbanks, G. Recent Experimental Investigations of Vocal pitch in Speech, *Journal of the Acoustical Society of America,* II, 1940.

Ferguson, C.A. & Chowdhury, M.Phonemes of Bengali, *Language*, Vol. 36, 1960, Baltimore.

Firth, J.R. *Papers in Linguistics,* London, 1957.

Ghatage, A.M. *Phonemic and Morphomic Frequencies in Hindi,* Poona, 1964.

Gleason, H.A. Jr. *Introduction to Descriptive Linguistics,* New York, 1958.

——, *Workbook in Descriptive Linguistics,* New York, 1955.

Grierson, G.A. *Linguistic Survey of India,* Vol.V, Part II, 1903.

——, Spontaneous Nasalization in the Indo-Aryan Languages. *JRAS,* 1922.

Harris, Zellig, S. *Structural Linguistics,* Chicago, 1947.

Heffner, R-M.S.*General Phonetics,* America, 1952.

Hockett, C.F. A *Course in Modern Linguistics,* New York, 1963.

——, *The Manual of Phonology,* Baltimore, 1955.

International Phonetic Association, The Principle of International Phonetic Association, London, 1961.

Jakobson, and Halle, M. *Fundamentals of Language,* S.Gravenhage, 1956.

Jakobson, R.Fant, G. and Halle, M. *Preliminaries to Speech Analysis,* Cambridge, 1955.

Jones, Daniel. *An Outline of English Phonetics,* Cambridge, 1962.

Joos, Martin. Readings in Linguistics, Washington, 1957.

——, *Acoustic Phonetics,* Baltimore, 1948.

Kelkar, A.R. The Phonology and Morphology of Marathi, (Unpublished Ph.D.Thesis, University of Cornell,1958.)

Khubchandani, L.M. The Phonology and Morpho phonemics of Sindhi. (Unpublished Thesis, Univ. of Pennsylvania, 1961.)

Malmberg,B. *Phonetics,* New York, 1963.

Martin, Samuel, E. Korean Phonemics, Readings in Linguistics, Washington, 1957.

Mehrotra, Ramesh Chandra. *Phonemes of Hindi, Indian Linguistics,* Vol.25, 1964.

——, *Hindi Syllabic Structure,* Indian Linguistics,Turner Jubilee Volume, 1959.

——, *Hindi me Balaghat Aur Surlahar,* RajRishi Tandan Abhinandan Granth.

Moulton, G.William. Juncture in Modern standard German, Readings in Linguistics, Washington, 1957.

Pandit P.B. Nasalization, Aspiration and Murmur in Gujarati, Indian Linguistics,*Taraporewala Memorial Volume,* 1957.

Pike, k.L. *Phonemics,* A Technique for reducing Language to writing. Michigan,1947.

——, *Phonetics, Michigan,* 1943.

——, *The Intonation of American English,* Michigan, 1958.

Potter, Kopp and Green. *Visible Speech,* New York, 1947.

prasad, B.N. *Magahi Sanskar Geet,* Patna, 1962.

——, *Kurmali Bhasha Aur Sahtiya,* Patna, 1960.

——, The Position of the Nasals in the Bhojpuri Phonological System, Indian Linguistics, 1955-56.

Prasad, Guru. Sandhayakshron ka Apurna Uccharan, *Nagari Pracharini Patrika,* Banaras.

Prasad, Seryoo. Magahī: Udgam tatha Vikas, *Parishad Patrika,* Patna, 1966.

Prasad, Swarnalata. Juncture and Aitch in Magahi, *Indian Linguistics,* Turner Jubilee Volume II, 1959.

Saksena, Babu Ram. *Evolution of Awadhi,* Allahabad, 1937.

Sankaran,C.R. Process of Speech, Poona, 1963.

Sankrityan, Rahul. *Magadhi ka Vikas,* Ganga Puratatwank, 1933.

Sapir, Edward. *Language,* New York, 1949.

Scripture, E.W. *Researches in Experimental Phonetics,* New York.

Smalley, A. William. Manual of Articulatory Phonetics,(two parts), New York, 1962-63.

Sourirajan S. and Sankaran, C.R. The Utterance-continum and the a Phoneme, *Bulletin of the Deccan college Postgraduate and Research Institute,* Vol.VI, Nos.1 and 2.

Stetson, R.H. Motor Phonetics, Amsterdam, 1951.

Sweet Henry, *A handbook of Phonetics,* oxford, 1877.

Tanakadata. A Study of the Japanese Phonemes by means of Tone Films, Proceedings of the Second International congress of Phonetic science, 1936.

Tiwari, Mahesh. *Pali Bhasha Aur Sahitya,* Patna, 1962.
Tiwari, U.N. Bhojpuri Bhasha Aur Sahitya, Patna, 1954.
——, *Bhasha Shastra ki Ruprekha.* Allahabad, 1963.
Verma, Dhirendra. *Hindi Bhasha ka Itihas,* Allahabad, 1958.
——, *Braj Bhasha,* Allahabad, 1954.
Verma, Siddheshwar. Nasalization in Hindi Literary Works, *Journal of Deptt. of Letters,* XVIII, Univ. of Calcutta,
Zipf, G.K. *The Psycho-biology of Language,* 1936.

Bibliography of Works on Magahī (in chronological order)

Campbell, G. : Specimens of Languages of India (Lists of words and sentences in the vernacular of Patna and Gaya), Calcutta, 1874.
Crierson, G.A. : Seven Grammars of the Dialects and sub-dialects of the Bihari Languages, Part III-VI, Calcutta, 1883 and 1886.
——, *Bihar Peasant Life,* Calcutta and London, 1885.
Hoernle, A.F.R., & Grierson, G.A. : A Comparative Dictionary of the Bihari Language, Part I,1885, Part II, 1889. Calcutta.
Kellogg, the Rev.S.H : A *Grammar of Hindi Language* (2nd edn. Rev. and Enlarged). London, 1893.
Grierson, G.A.: *Linguistic Survey of India,* Vol.V, Part II, 1903.
Sankrityana, Rahul : *Magadhi ka Vikas,* Ganga Puratatwank, 1933.
——, *Hindi Sahitya ka Brihat Itihas,* Vol.XVI, (pp.39-81) V.S.2017.
Singh, Kapildeo : *Magahi Bhasha Aur Sahitya,* Sahitya,Patna, January, 1952.
Singh, Uma : Maghi Lok kathayon ka Adhyayan, (unpublished thesis for M.A.Patna University, 1959-61).
Prasad, Nageshwar : *Magahi Boli,* Prachi, May, 1952. Monghyr.
Tiwari, U.N.: *Bhojpuri Bhasha Aur Sahitya,* (pp.169-201, 217-227), Patna, 1954.
Prasad, Krishnadeo : *Magahai Bhasha Aur Sahitya,* Patna, 1957.

Sashtri, Ramasankar. Magahi (A Paper Presented for Reading in the first Session of Bihar Magahi-Mandal At Yekangarsarai), 1957.

Jha, Subhadra : *The Formation of the Maithili Language,* (Introduction),London, 1958.

Yodhey, Rajendra Kumar : *Magahi Vyakaran,* Patna, 1958.

Diwakar, R.R. : Bihar Through the Ages, (Chap.III pp.85-90, Chap.XI pp.347-357), Govt.of Bihar,1958.

Prasad, B.N. & Jha Sudhaker Shastri : Linguistic Survey of Sadar Sub-division of Manbhum and Dhalbhum (Singbhum), Patna, 1958.

Bajpeyee, Kishori Das: *Hindi Shabdanushasan,* Varanasi, 1958.

Prasad, B.N. : *Krishi kosh,* Patna, 1959.

——, *Kurmali Bhasha Aur Sahitya,* Patna, 1960.

——, *Magahi Sanskar Geet,* Patna, 1962.

Yogeshwar : *Magahi me Urdu Shabda,* Bhasha, New Delhi, September, 1963.

Aryani, Sampatti : *Magahi Vyakaran kosh,* Patna, 1965.

Shreekanta,Ramakant Mishra : Patna Aur Gaya Zile me Boli jane bali Magahi Bhasha ka Aitihasik Adhyyan, (unpublished thesis for Ph.D.Patna,Univ.1965).

——, *Magahi Bhasha ke Utpatti*, Bihan, Patna, April, 1965.

Prasad, Saryoo : Magahi : Udgam Tatha Vikas,Parishad Patrika, Patna, 1966.

Prasad, Swarnalata. Juncture and Aitch in Magahi, *Indian Linguistics,* Turner Jubilee Volume II, 1959.

INDEX